*Presented To:*

_____

❦

*From:*

_____

❦

*Date:*

_____

# Daybreak with God

eagle

Guildford, Surrey

Copyright © 1999 Honor Books

Originally published by Honor Books, PO Box 55388, Tulsa, Oklahoma 74155, USA. This edition published 2000 by Eagle Publishing Ltd, PO Box 530, Guildford, Surrey GU2 4FH.

British Library Cataloguing in Publication Data. A catalogue record for this book is available from the British Library.

Manuscript written and compiled by Robert J. Exley, Marla M. Patterson, Patti M. Hummel and Gayle S. Edwards.

Typeset by Eagle Publishing
Printed by Cox & Wyman
ISBN: 0 86347 377 6

*Daybreak with God*

# Morning by Morning

*O God, you are my God, I seek you.*
Psalm 63:1 NRSV

*Great is Thy faithfulness, Oh God my Father!*
*Morning by morning, new mercies I see.*
*All I have needed, thy hands hath provided.*
*Great is thy faithfulness, Lord, unto me.*
*(Traditional Hymn)*

*T*here's something fresh and new about the beginning of each day. As sun filters through the trees, as birds begin their morning song, as day dawns, there is a new awareness of God's hand at work in our hearts and lives. Yesterday is past; tomorrow is still a day away. But today offers a new beginning – here and now.

*O LORD, in the morning you hear my voice;*
*in the morning I lay my requests before you*
*and wait in expectation.*
*Psalm 5:3*

Throughout Scripture, the Lord invites us to spend time with Him before we face the demands of our lives. He urges His children to seek Him first, to give our best to Him first, to ask Him first.

Why? Because we need Him. And knowing that we need Him is always a good place to start any day.

Just like a good night's sleep refreshes the body, so a quiet moment with God at daybreak revitalizes our spirits before the day's responsibilities descend upon us. Starting the day with a holy hush before the morning rush can make the difference between a day wasted and a day well lived.

*Rejoicing comes in the morning.*
*Psalm 30:5*

No matter what happened yesterday, you have today. It is a gift from your Heavenly Father. Open your heart to a quiet moment with God. May these gentle, joyful devotionals help you celebrate your faith in God, renew your mind, refresh your spirit and encourage your heart.

☙

## *Living Beyond the Thunder*

*Be strong and take heart, all you who
hope in the LORD.*
Psalm 31:24

In *The Diary of a Young Girl*, Anne
Frank wrote, 'I simply can't build up my
hopes on a foundation consisting of confusion, misery, and death.'[1] She understood
that hope originates somewhere beyond our
immediate circumstances. In fact, hope –
real hope – often stands alone in the darkness.

How was this young girl capable of
courage and faith far beyond her years?
She refused to allow the devastation of her
times to shape her view of life. In her
words, 'It's really a wonder that I haven't
dropped all my ideals . . . Yet I keep them.
I hear the ever-approaching thunder. I can
feel the sufferings of millions and yet, if I
look up into the heavens, I think that it will
all come right.'[2]

We can't know what horrors Anne Frank

8

and her family suffered in the Holocaust, but we do know only her father emerged alive. Yet her words live on. Decades later, several generations have read and been touched by the diary of a young girl facing one of the darkest periods in world history – a girl who chose hope in the midst of hopelessness.

Life sometimes includes hardship. When tests come, we have the same choice Anne Frank had: hold onto our ideals or drop them. When life circumstances sound like 'approaching thunder', remember the simple truth in the life of a young Jewish girl. A foundation made of the right ingredients makes for an overcoming life. Holding tightly to one's ideals no matter the circumstance is a hallmark of character.

*In all things God works for the good of those who love him, who have been called according to his purpose.*
*Romans 8:28*

આ

# Holy Hush

*But you, O Lord, are a compassionate and
gracious God, slow to anger, abounding in
love and faithfulness.*
Psalm 86:15

All is still as a man sits at his dining-
room table allowing the pages of a well-worn
Bible to slip slowly through his fingers,
basking in the peace of the moment. The
pages have a comfortable feel and the soft
plop they make as they fall barely disturbs
the quiet. Early morning always brings
with it a hush of holiness for him. In his
mind's eye he remembers another such
morning.

The new dawn air is tangy and sharp as
he and his brother turn onto a gravel road
bordered by wheat fields. Early in the
growing season the wheat is about two feet
high and a brilliant green. Suddenly the
boy catches his breath. From the edge of
the field, a ring-necked pheasant comes into

view just as a bright ray of sunshine creates a natural spotlight. As if showing off for God Himself, the pheasant stops and strikes a pose.

Time stands still, sound ceases and God paints an image on the young boy's brain that will remain for a lifetime. The beautiful hues of the pheasant with its shining white collar glistening in the sunshine against the vivid green of the wheat remains sharply etched in his memory. Whenever he relives that day, he experiences anew the presence of God and a supernatural sense of content-ment. Slowly the memory recedes, but the presence of God remains.

Sir Thomas Brown said, 'Nature is the art of God.' All around us are awesome reminders of a big God who created every-thing in a matter of days. Isn't it great to know the artist firsthand?

 CR

# The Fisherman

*But godliness actually is a means of great gain,*
*when accompanied by contentment.*
*1 Timothy 6:6 NASB*

A wealthy man spent his days fishing in the lake beside his mansion. Every day, on the same lake he saw a poor man who lived in a rickety shack. The poor man fished with a stick and some string. He sat only an hour or so, rarely catching more than two fish, then went home.

The years passed and, frustrated from too much thinking, the rich man approached the poor: 'Please excuse me, but we've seen each other fishing here for years, and I'm curious. You sit here every day catching only a few fish and then heading home. I couldn't help but wonder why you don't stay longer.

'You see, if you just stayed one or two hours more each day, you could sell your extra fish in town. You could get enough money for a better fishing rod, then catch more fish. You could eventually get a boat and a net. Then with even more fish, you could hire another man and another boat. Soon you would not even have to be on the boats all day; you could have a huge company earning a lot of money. Then, you could easily spend your days fishing alone, for only as long as you would like, doing what you want with no worries.'

'But, sir, I don't understand,' said the poor man, 'that's what I do now.'[3]

To be content with the life God has given us is to live the richest life of all.

∝

# A Time to Pray

*He has made everything appropriate in its time.*
*Ecclesiastes 3:11 NASB*

Several years ago a television advertise-
ment focused on a lovely young woman's
smiling face. She was looking down and
obviously very busy at the task before her,
although what she was doing was not
shown. At the same time she was doing this
task she was praying. The ad's emphasis
was on taking time to pray no matter what
else we must do during the day.

As the camera moved away from this
young woman's face and down to what she
was doing, it became clear that this was a
young mother changing her baby's nappy.

What a lovely picture of how easy it is
for us to talk with the Lord. Setting a
chunk of time aside every morning might
not work every day for you, but during
each twenty-four-hour day we can creatively find a portion of time that is just for God.

*We mutter and sputter,*
*We fume and we spurt,*
*We mumble and grumble,*
*Our feelings get hurt.*
*We can't understand things,*
*Our vision grows dim,*
*When all that we need is:*
*A moment with Him.*[4]

Most of us are so busy during the day that we find it increasingly difficult to set aside time to spend in prayer, not just a quick prayer of thanks, but a time of genuine communication with the Lord.

God wants this time with us and we need it with Him. There are times we can be alone with the Saviour, but we need to creatively look for them.

## Wake-Up Call

*Awake to righteousness, and sin not.*
*1 Corinthians 15:34 KJV*

Boot camp was a rude awakening for a young man who entered the army to get away from his parents' rules. He reasoned that going into the service would give him the freedom he wanted to do whatever he pleased. He knew boot camp would be tough, but he was certain he could handle it. Besides, it only lasted for six weeks. After that he would be free!

Upon waking that first morning to his sergeant's yells, the young soldier came face to face with the reality that mum, dad and all his teachers clumped together couldn't compare to what he was about to face. His six weeks loomed as an eternity. He regularly wrote to his family and included the first thank-you notes his parents had ever received from their son. He even expressed thanks for what his teachers had done for him.

This young soldier found out quickly the importance of learning how to handle what could attack a soldier in war. He was faced with a reason to wake up and a reason to be prepared. The sergeant trained the young recruits to anticipate the enemy's strategy, making certain they knew the enemy was lurking and ready to attack without warning. He taught them that the enemy is extremely cunning and watches and waits for your weakest, most vulnerable time to attack.

The Bible tells us to awake to righteousness and to prepare ourselves, so we will not sin. God has provided the right armour and training required to defeat the enemy. We become soldiers for Christ when we join His family. God's enemies are our enemies, and the battle is over the most precious of God's creations: the human soul.

CR

# The Importance of Everyday Talk

*Let your conversation be always full of grace.*
Colossians 4:6

The banquet hall is festively adorned with beautiful flowers and ribbons. Across the front of the room a large banner reads, 'A Golden Congratulations for a Golden Couple'. It is their fiftieth wedding anniversary, and family and friends have gathered from far and near to pay tribute to them. The four children each take a turn at describing their fondest memories and greatest lessons learned from their parents. Then the cake is cut, pictures are taken and everyone enjoys being together.

Too soon, the afternoon draws to a conclusion. Friends say goodbye; family members repack mementos in the cars and everyone leaves. Later that evening, one of the grandchildren asks, 'What is the secret, Grandma, to being happily married for fifty years?' Without hesitation, her grandmother replies, 'We were always able to talk about everything.'

Recent research supports her conclusion. A study of couples happily married for more than twenty-five years found only one thing they all had in common – each couple 'chitchatted' with each other daily. Perhaps, since they already know how to converse with one another, they are more able to talk out their differences when tough times come. The same most likely holds true for our relationship with God. If we commune with Him regularly, then we will automatically turn to Him first when crisis comes.

Have you had a quiet time talking with God today?

☙

# Good Morning, Lord

*In the morning, O LORD, Thou wilt hear my voice;*
*in the morning I will order my prayer to Thee*
*and eagerly watch.*
*Psalm 5:3 NASB*

There is something extraordinarily special about early morning devotions. Before the hectic day begins with its noise and numerous distractions, there is usually a calm that is uncommon to any other time of the day, a peaceful prerequisite for entering into the prayer closet with Christ. Christ set an example for us when He rose up early and prayed.

Morning is the first step to the list of 'things to do' written out the night before and a world of unknown plans prepared by God for us to become acquainted with. Morning is a wonderfully private time where intimate conversation and gentle responses can take place between God and His children. This is a time to listen to the very heart of God.

Oswald Chambers said, 'Get an inner
chamber in which to pray where no one
knows you are praying, shut the door, and
talk to God in secret. Have no other motive
than to know your Father in heaven. It is
impossible to conduct your life as a disciple
without definite times of secret prayer.'

*Between Midnight and Morning*
*You that have faith to look with fearless eyes*
*Beyond the tragedy of a world of strife,*
*And trust that out of night and death shall rise*
*The dawn of ampler life;*
*Rejoice, whatever anguish rend your heart,*
*That God has given you, for a priceless dower,*
*To live in these great times and have your part*
*In Freedom's crowning hour;*
*That we may tell your sons who see the light*
*High in heaven — their heritage to take —*
*'I saw the powers of darkness put to flight!*
*I saw the morning break!'*
   – Owen Seaman

**CR**

# *The Art of Caring*

*And now these three remain: faith, hope and love.*
*But the greatest of these is love.*
*1 Corinthians 13:13*

This was the first meeting of a support group for middle school youngsters who had suffered significant losses in their lives. The group leader was unsure of what to expect, so the question really caught him by surprise.

'Why does God kill babies?'

The question hung in the air for an eternity, and two young faces stared intently at the group counsellor waiting for an answer. He gazed at the two brothers' faces as he contemplated how to respond. He wished to reassure them that God does not kill babies, yet, for the moment, the answer to the question seemed far less important than what prompted it.

'Something really sad must have happened for you guys to ask such a question,' he finally responded.

The two brothers shared the sad story of how their entire family had hoped for a new baby. The boys badly wanted to become uncles. Finally, their older sister became pregnant, but the baby was still-born. They could not understand why this would happen.

With careful encouragement and much listening, the counsellor found a way for the two brothers to come to grips with the loss of their niece. Although it eventually became understood that her death was not a direct act of God, they still struggled with why it happened.

As the other group members shared their own stories of loss and sadness, a kinship developed among the group that lifted the sadness. It seems that once people allow themselves to honestly share one another's sadness, then the darkness cannot remain.

Psychologist Rollo May said, 'Care is a state in which something does matter; it is the source of human tenderness.' Take time to care every chance you get!

## *The Good Life*

*Whom have I in heaven but Thee? And besides*
*Thee, I desire nothing on earth.*
*My flesh and my heart*
*may fail, but God is the strength of*
*my heart and my portion forever.*
*Psalm 73:25, 26 NASB*

*A* popular Internet joke goes something
like this:

A secretary, a paralegal and a partner in
a big law firm are walking to lunch when
they find an antique oil lamp.

They rub it and a genie comes out in a
puff of smoke. The genie says, 'I usually
only grant three wishes, so I'll give each of
you just one.'

'Me first!' says the secretary. 'I want to
be in the Bahamas, driving a speedboat,
without a care in the world.'

Poof! She's gone.

'Me next!' says the paralegal. 'I want to
be in Hawaii, relaxing on the beach with

my personal masseuse, an endless supply of
piña coladas, and the love of my life.'

Poof! He's gone.

'You're next,' the genie says to the partner. The partner says, 'I want those two
back in the office right after lunch.'

We've been told for ages that we can
'have it all'. But there's too much to do, not
enough time – and no magic lamp to do it
for us. And we wouldn't even want it all if
we didn't think it would make us happy.

However, those in the know say there's
an easier path to a happy life. These three
simple thoughts are cited as the keys to
happiness:

1) Fret not – He loves you (John 13:1).
2) Faint not – He holds you (Psalm
   139:10).
3) Fear not – He keeps you (Psalm
   121:5).

It is possible to have it all . . . by making
God your 'all'.

CR

# *Morning Praise!*

*Come before Him with joyful singing.*
*Psalm 100:2 NASB*

A young career woman moved away from her home to New York City. She rented a room from an elderly lady who had migrated to the United States years before from Sweden. The landlady offered a clean room, a shared bathroom and use of the kitchen at a reasonable rate.

The little white-haired Swedish woman made the rules of the house very clear. There would be no smoking or drinking, no food in the bedrooms, etc. Pausing mid-sentence, the landlady asked, 'Do you sing? Do you play? Music is good! I used to play the piano at the church, but not now. I'm too old. My hearing isn't good, but I love to praise God with music. God loves music.'

After a full day of moving into her new room, the young tenant slept soundly until 5:30 am when she was jarred awake by horrible noises coming from somewhere downstairs. Cautiously making her way down the stairway, she followed the sounds to the kitchen door. There she discovered her new landlady standing at the stove, dressed for the day, joyfully 'singing' at the top of her lungs!

Never had the young woman heard such a horrible voice. Yet she heard that voice, precious to God, start every morning off the same way for as long as she rented the room just over the kitchen.

The Swedish lady passed into glory a few years later. The tenant moved on, married and had her own family. She is alone now also, and has lost some of her hearing. Yet, every morning finds her standing in front of the stove, singing off key and loud, but joyful, praises to the Lord!

A glorious way to start the day!

CR

# *Hay Fields and Special Friends*

*But it is you, a man like myself, my companion,
my close friend.*
*Psalm 55:13*

The predawn air had a distinct chill to it when the pickup truck horn sounded each morning that summer. Rob would wander out to the truck where Ben Roy waited. Farmers would hire Ben Roy, with his New Holland hay stacker, to collect the baled hay from their fields and build large square haystacks for feeding the livestock during winter.

The work itself was always the same, but the ease of doing it varied tremendously because of the type of hay. Alfalfa made tight, hard bales that were easy to handle. Wheat made looser bales that were apt to break apart and thus were much more work.

First thing, Rob would ask, 'Are we

working wheat again today?' He always hoped for alfalfa, but without fail, it seemed, Ben would respond, 'Yep, wheat it is.' Rob would then doze until they arrived at the fields. Once there, they would enjoy a cup of coffee and watch the sun rise into the still morning air before the long day of hard work. Neither said much during those times, nor was it necessary.

Ben is retired and Rob has a family of his own, so they rarely see one another now. But when they do, it doesn't take long for the conversation to turn to that special summer. Each man recalls different lessons learned from their work together, but a common one is their shared belief that finding God's will requires a commitment to serving Him no matter how hard – or easy – the work.

God's presence is like that. It's not what is said or not said that matters so much as it is the being together and the lessons we learn.

☙❧

## *Lasting Legacies*

*Good will come to him who is generous and lends freely, who conducts his affairs with justice.*
Psalm 112:5

*M*arian Wright Edelman, attorney and founding president of the Children's Defense Fund, often speaks of how Martin Luther King had a profound impact on her life. All Americans have been affected by Dr King's life in some way and few have not heard his famous comment, 'I have a dream'. But it was not his public persona that had an impact upon her; it was his willingness to admit his fears.

She writes, 'I remember him as someone able to admit how often he was afraid and unsure about his next step . . . It was his human vulnerability and his ability to rise above it that I most remember.'

She should know about rising above fear and uncertainty because her life has not been an easy one, and one wonders just how often she has drawn strength from the self-honesty and candour of Dr King.

Ms Edelman grew up during the days of segregation, one of five children, the daughter of a Baptist minister. She graduated from Spelman College and Yale University Law School and was the first black woman to pass the bar in the state of Mississippi. She is a prolific and gifted writer and has devoted her life to serving as an activist for disadvantaged Americans, especially children.

Hers is an incredible testimony to the belief in helping others to help themselves. She never doubted that she could make a difference. 'I have always believed that I could help change the world because I have been lucky to have adults around me who did – in small and large ways.'

We have the same opportunity. Will we respond as well as she? Will we help change the world?

CR

# Great Beginnings

> *'Let your light so shine before men, that they*
> *may see your good works and glorify your*
> *Father in heaven.'*
> *Matthew 5:16 NKJV*

*I*n his best-seller, *The Seven Habits of Highly Effective People*, Stephen Covey entitles one of the seven habits as 'Begin with the End in Mind'. He uses an illustration of imagining yourself at your own funeral. If you close your eyes and imagine the people in attendance, the flowers, the music and the minister delivering the eulogy, how would it go if your life were to end today?

How would you want it to be?

Through his illustration, Covey demonstrates that, in order to achieve a goal, we must have that goal in mind in everything we do along the way.

More importantly, everything we do today – whether in line with our long-range desires or not – affects what we become for

the rest of our lives. And what we become
affects everyone whose lives we touch.
What a ripple effect! There's an old
Chinese proverb that says:

> *If there is light in the soul,*
> *There will be beauty in the person.*
> *If there is beauty in the person,*
> *There will be harmony in the house.*
> *If there is harmony in the house,*
> *There will be order in the nation.*
> *If there is order in the nation,*
> *There will be peace in the world.*

If you remember the 1970s, you'll recog-
nise the phrase, 'Today is the first day of
the rest of your life'. Today is our opportunity to begin with the end in mind. If we
begin with God's light in our souls, we can
bring beauty, harmony, order, and peace –
the Prince of Peace – to the world.

СЗ

## *Just the Facts*

*He that is void of wisdom despiseth his neighbour:*
*but a man of understanding holdeth his peace.*
*Proverbs 11:12 KJV*

There was once a man that John Wesley thought of as miserly, therefore he had little respect for him. He felt so strongly about this man that, on an occasion when the man gave only a small gift to a worthy charity, Wesley openly criticized him.

Not long afterwards, the gentleman paid a visit to Wesley. He was surprised to hear that this man – someone whom he assumed was simply greedy – had actually been living on parsnips and water for several weeks. The man told him that, in his past, he had amassed a great deal of debt. But since his conversion, he had made a choice to pay off all of his creditors, and therefore was buying nothing for himself and spending as little as possible elsewhere in order to do so.

'Christ has made me an honest man,' he said, 'and so with all these debts to pay, I can give only a few offerings above my tithe. I must settle up with my worldly neighbours and show them what the grace of God can do in the heart of a man who was once dishonest.'

Wesley then apologized to the man and asked his forgiveness.[5]

It's easy to find fault with others when we don't know their circumstances or the reasons for their actions. It's also amazing how a few facts can forever alter our perception of a situation. When we feel compelled to judge, it's a good time to ask God for wisdom and patience to understand the facts.

☙

## My Heart for You

*Therefore, as God's chosen people, holy and
dearly loved, clothe yourselves with compassion,
kindness, humility, gentleness and patience.*
Colossians 3:12

There is a story told of the famous
escape artist Harry Houdini that gives a
glimpse into his heart.

Early in his career when he was still an
unknown vaudeville act, he and his young
wife were living from week to week with no
reserves of food or money. One afternoon
he ventured out to the marketplace to purchase groceries. Within a few minutes he
returned and sat at the kitchen table weep-
ing uncontrollably.

Uncertain what had happened, but fear-
ing the worst, his wife tried to console him
and to find out what had occurred. Finally,
controlling his sobs, Harry related to her
that he had not been harmed nor assaulted.
It seems that on his way to the market, he

came across a young man who was crippled and begging for food. Harry immediately gave the man all that he had and then returned to the apartment.

Why then was Harry crying? He had done a very noble thing. Perhaps he was upset because he was too impulsive and now he and his wife had nothing left for them. No, he was not crying for them. He was crying because he had no more to give.

Harry Houdini demonstrated the greatest gift of all that day. He exhibited empathy, and it is empathy that keeps our hearts fresh and new. Thousands of years ago Homer said it like this:

> *Yet, taught by time, my heart has learned to glow*
> *For others' good, and melt at others' woe.*

CR

# The Invitation

*And the son said unto him, Father,
I . . . am no more worthy to be called thy son.*
*Luke 15:21 KJV*

Rita stood on the pavement peering
wistfully at the beautiful home. Through
the curtained windows she saw nicely
dressed people chatting with one another
and enjoying refreshments. In her hand she
clutched an engraved, personal invitation to
the dinner party. She had been invited to
attend this evening's affair by her professor
who was impressed with her academic abil-
ities and wanted her to meet others at the
university.

She carefully fingered the invitation,
looked down at her nice 'party dress' which
seemed so dull and ordinary in comparison
to the gowns she saw through the window,
and with a sadness of the soul she turned
and slowly walked away. Clutched between
her fingers: the unused invitation.

This poignant and painful scene from the British film *Educating Rita* demonstrates just how difficult it is for one to accept the possibility of a new life. Rita came from a lower middle class family, and no one had attended university before her. She struggled with feelings of inadequacy and was forever wondering how she would 'fit in'. It is this sense of self-doubt that caused her to fail to take action on the invitation.

However, thanks to a persistent professor, who saw more in her than she saw in herself, she eventually accepted his invitation to join a new world. By the film's end, this once modest woman excels as a scholar.

The invitation to become and then excel as a Christian is for each of us. The greatest joy, though, is in knowing that our Master Teacher always sees much more in us than we usually see in ourselves.

God does not ask about our ability, but our availability.

CR

## A New Look

*Happy are the people who are in such a state;*
*Happy are the people whose God is the LORD!*
*Psalm 144:15 NKJV*

In 1998, twenty-one-year-old Se Ri Pak became the newest 'wonder kid' of women's professional golf, winning the US Open and later becoming the first woman to shoot 61 in an LPGA event. Having played golf for only six years before turning professional, her amazing ascent was attributed not only to talent, but also to a fierce mental focus based in the Asian tradition of controlling one's emotions.

Onlookers are awed at the young player's ability to ignore distractions on the course. Even her caddy was asked if they were fighting because she walks alone and does not talk with him. But it's because she is intensely focused all the time.

In fact, her control is such that Se Ri broke into tears for the first time in her life upon winning the US Open. Emotional display is that unusual for her. But she explains how she's working to change that habit:

*I usually look very serious, but after I started playing golf at 14, I saw Nancy Lopez on TV. I didn't know she was a great golfer — all I knew was that she always smiled. My goal is to be that way too. Now when I sign autographs, I always put a smile by my name . . . Even if I don't win, I want to give people a smile.*[6]

It is said a smile is the best way to improve your appearance. It's also one of the nicest things you can do for others. Pass it on!

## Breakfast Guest

*'Come and have breakfast.'*
John 21:12 NASB

It was at sunrise when the men
returned from an all-night fishing trip, and
they had nothing to show for their efforts.
Not a single fish. As the boat approached
the shore, the men noticed a man calling to
them. He wanted to know if they had any
fish.

The tired fishermen answered that they
did not. The man then told them to cast
their nets on the right side of their boat.
When they did as the man on the shore
suggested, the net was immediately filled
with large fish.

One of the fishermen was John, a disciple of Christ. He recognized the man on the
shore. It was the Lord. The disciples knew
Jesus because they had spent time with
Him and they recognized Him from a distance. When they reached shore Jesus had

a charcoal fire already laid with fish cooking and bread ready. He invited the disciples to bring more fish from their catch and join Him for breakfast.

Can you imagine having breakfast with Christ? Think of what it would be like to have Him sitting across from you at your breakfast table. What kind of preparations would you make? What would you wear? Who would you tell? What would you serve? Would you be on tenterhooks getting ready, wanting everything to be perfect?

Christ is ready with an RSVP to pass back immediately he receives our invitation to Him. He is delighted to join us for breakfast, or any meal – anytime!

&

# The Magic of Instructions

*Pay attention and listen to the sayings of the wise.*
Proverbs 22:17

Angrily the young man flung his wrench across the driveway and rolled away from the car. He had been trying for hours to change the brake pads on his wife's small car. It didn't help matters that he was at best a 'mediocre' mechanic. Finally, in exasperation he stormed into the house and informed his wife that something was seriously wrong with her car and he could not fix it.

'In fact,' he shouted, 'I don't know if anyone can fix it!'

She quietly thanked him for his efforts and then moved to the telephone where she called her father, a master mechanic. After she explained the situation, she and her father ventured to the nearest library where they found a manual for her car. They carefully made copies of the pages giving directions on how to change the brake pads. Next, they stopped at a car auto parts shop and purchased a small but vital tool necessary for this particular job. Finally, they proceeded home to her car and within thirty minutes the repair job was complete.

What made the difference? Three things: first, she contacted her father, a master mechanic. The first instruction God gives us is to call upon Him. Second, they found the right set of instructions and carefully followed them. Sometimes, we insist on trying to do things without consulting the instructions. Finally, they secured the proper tool to do the job. God will always give us the right tool if we will just go and secure it.

Whether we are talking about brake pads or critical life decisions, it is simply amazing – almost magical – how well things work out when we follow instructions.

CR

## More than Atoms

*But let each one examine his own work, and then
he will have rejoicing in himself alone, and
not in another.*
*Galatians 6:4 NKJV*

*T*wo young brothers were engaged in
their ongoing battle for sibling superiority.
Adam, aged nine, was explaining to four-
year-old Rob the science of living matter,
taking no small pleasure in his advantage of
a primary school education.

Soon, a skirmish broke out, with cries of
'Am not!' and 'Are too!' ringing through
the house. Rob ran crying to find his mother.

'Mu-u-u-m . . . is everything made of
atoms?'

'Yes, that's true . . .'

'But he said *I'm* made of atoms!'

'Sweetie, he's right. Everything in the
world is made of atoms.'

Rob sank to the floor, sobbing as if his

heart had broken. His perplexed mum picked him up and hugged him. 'What on earth is the matter?'

'It's not fair!' he howled. 'I don't want to be made of Adams – I want to be made of *Robs*!'

We all want recognition for our 'specialness'. But we should never take our selfworth from our society, feedback from others, or our own comparisons to others. Our self-esteem should be based in the fact that God created us with the utmost care and has called His creation good.[7]

In His foresight we are all made of 'the right stuff'. Our self-worth then comes from how we use it, in service to our families and communities, exercising our creative gifts and becoming one with God. No amount of stature in the eyes of man can equal the reward of following God's will. That's how we grow into more than just a collection of atoms!

CR

## As Time Goes By

*This is the day which the LORD has made;*
*we will rejoice and be glad in it.*
*Psalm 118:24 NKJV*

'Where does the time go?' we ask. Here it is – a new day on the horizon – and we can't remember how it arrived so quickly. Why, last week seems like yesterday, and last year flew by like a video in fast-forward.

And worse, it's hard to remember what we spent it on.

Shouldn't I have more great memories?

What did I accomplish?

Is this all I've done with all that time?

Singer Jim Croce mused in his hit song *Time in a Bottle* that 'there never seems to be enough time to do the things you want to do, once you find them'. We search so hard for happiness. But often we don't understand that happiness is not a goal to be won, but a by-product of a life well spent.

This 'Old English Prayer' offers simple instruction for enjoying the day that the Lord has made:

*Take time to work, it is the price of success.*
*Take time to think, it is the source of power.*
*Take time to play, it is the secret of*
*perpetual youth.*
*Take time to read, it is the foundation of wisdom.*
*Take time to be friendly, it is the road to*
*happiness.*
*Take time to dream, it is hitching your wagon*
*to a star.*
*Take time to love and be loved, it is the privilege*
*of the gods.*
*Take time to look around, it is too short a day*
*to be selfish.*
*Take time to laugh, it is the music of the soul.*

ଔ

## A New Song

*He put a new song in my mouth, a hymn of*
*praise to our God.*
*Psalm 40:3*

Singer and songwriter Bobby Michaels
tells how one summer he sensed a growing
hunger to come up with a new song, but he
could not find it within him. As he was visiting his publishing company to discuss a
new album, he met a young man working
as an assistant. The young man mentioned
that he wrote songs, and Bobby found himself pouring his heart out to the young man.

'Forget what might be appealing or what
might sell,' said the young man. 'Just tell
me what you think God wants you to sing
about.' Bobby's story inspired the young
man to write a beautiful song that uncannily
communicated Bobby's heart. The name of
the song is 'My Redeemer Is Faithful and
True'. It is an unpretentious and simple
prayer of thanksgiving to our Creator. It is

a reverent statement of faith in God's faithfulness. It literally made Bobby's heart sing
anew his love for his Saviour.

The sales staff and editors did not like
the song. In fact, they did not believe that it
would sell. 'Too slow,' they said. 'Too
redundant.' On and on they went. But
Bobby remained adamant that this song
was directly from God and that it was
anointed of God. It ministered to him, and
it would minister to others.

Guess what? Bobby was right. God has
used the song to bless countless numbers of
individuals, and the testimony he gives at
his concerts prior to singing the song makes
thousands of hearts sing right along with
him. And the young man who wrote the
song was Steven Curtis Chapman, winner
of numerous Dove and Grammy awards.

Isn't God simply amazing! What new
song does He want to put in your heart
today?

CR

## *I Can See Clearly Now*

*We know that, when He appears, we shall be like*
*Him, because we shall see Him just as He is.*
*1 John 3:2 NASB*

Between Macon and Valdosta, Georgia,
lies a stretch of highway, Interstate 75,
known for heavy fog that causes massive
pileups of cars, vans, trucks and campers.
Several times each year horrible accidents
happen as drivers enter the thick fog. Many
can't even see the front of their own vehi-
cle, much less beyond.

The result is a disaster waiting to happen
– and often it does. Many people are
injured, vehicles are destroyed and
motorists are delayed for hours. The costs
to personal property, the city and state, as
well as the increase in insurance rates are
astronomical. The worst tragedy is the loss
of human life.

Drivers involved in one of these accidents will tell you the same story. They saw

the fog but didn't think it was as thick as it turned out to be. They hoped to pass through it safely by turning their hazard lights on and driving slowly. These drivers had no idea that many vehicles in front of them had already been forced to stop — often victims of whatever tragedy had occurred to a car or lorry ahead of them.

In this life, we may see things through a fog of sin or circumstances. But the day will come when we can stand before Christ, and we will see Him clearly just as He is, in all His glory. Nothing will be able to cloud the true and living Christ from our vision when we go to heaven

The good news is that we don't have to wait. Today, right now, we can see Him clearly through His Word and in the lives of our godly brothers and sisters.

☙

## Book Me, Papaw!

*Children's children are the crown of old men;*
*and the glory of children are their fathers.*
*Proverbs 17:6 KJV*

*H*is eyes moistened with unbidden tears as Nicole climbed onto his lap and settled comfortably against his chest. Her hair, freshly shampooed and dried, smelled of lemons and touched his cheek, soft as down. With clear blue-green eyes, she looked expectantly up at his face, thrust the trusted and well-worn book of children's stories at him and said, 'Book me, Papaw, book me!'

'Papaw' James carefully adjusted his reading glasses, cleared his throat, and began the familiar story. She knew the words by heart and excitedly 'read' along with him. Every now and then he missed a word: she politely corrected him. 'No, Papaw, that's not what it says. Now let's do it again so that we get it right.'

She had no idea how her purity of heart thrilled his soul or how her simple trust in him moved him. James' was a far different childhood – one characterized by a harsh existence, made harder still by a distant and demanding father. His father ordered him to work the fields from dawn to dusk beginning in his fifth year of life. His child-hood memories sometimes continue to create anger and pain.

This first grandchild, though, has brought joy and light into his life in a way that supersedes his own childhood. He returns her love and faith with a gentleness and devotion that make her world secure and safe beyond measure. Theirs is a rela-tionship made for a lifetime. For Nicole, it lays a foundation for life. For James, it heals a past of pain.

'Book me, Papaw, book me!'

James Dobson sums it up well when he says, 'Children are not casual guests in our home.'[8]

## Without Words

*Show proper respect to everyone.*
*1 Peter 2:17*

As with many memorials, the Franklin Delano Roosevelt memorial in Washington, DC, came into being after years of debate. Women's groups demanded that his wife Eleanor be given appropriate recognition. Activists for the disabled ardently believed that FDR should be portrayed in his wheelchair. On and on, the debates raged. Finally, in spite of all the controversy, it was completed.

The memorial gives testimony to the fact that President Roosevelt and his wife Eleanor served America during some of its darkest years. It is a fitting design, for as visitors approach it, nothing really stands out. All one sees is a flat granite wall, perhaps twenty feet in height, with a simple quote from FDR; but this is just the beginning.

The memorial stretches directly away from the entrance. After rounding the wall, visitors move from area to area; every one marked by unique stillness. Each succeeding area is creatively set apart from the previous one making it a tribute in its own right. Visitors find themselves looking at human-sized sculptures of men and women standing in breadlines, reading quotes decrying the savagery of war, staring eye to eye with Eleanor Roosevelt and eventually looking up and across to see FDR in his wheelchair with his Scottish terrier beside him.

The strength of the memorial comes from its ability to draw the visitor into the presence of one man's passionate belief in serving his country. The impact of the memorial is to make each visitor more aware of the awesome responsibility of leadership – not just the leadership of presidents, but leadership of all people.

Whenever you have doubts about your purpose, remember the words of Martin Luther King, Jr., 'Everyone can be great because everyone can serve.'

CR

## *You Are One of Us*

*And be ye kind one to another, tenderhearted,*
*forgiving one another.*
*Ephesians 4:32 KJV*

'It's all right, sometimes I don't know why I do things either. You are part of our group, and we support you.' With that one statement, the tension evaporated from the room, and other teens expressed their support to Sara.

The setting was a community meeting of adolescents in a mental health treatment centre. Sara suffered from chronic schizophrenia and she often could not comprehend her actions or control them. The previous evening, upon returning from a visit home, she had promptly set a small fire in her bathroom that created major problems for the centre, including an evacuation and cancelling of evening activities.

The next morning, the staff and patients met to work through the problems of Sara's actions and the anger it created among the other teens. For nearly an hour she sat mute in the group as everyone tried to get her to explain. She would not meet anyone's eyes.

But when Sam, another patient, came across the room, knelt down before her, looked up into her face and expressed his support for her, she responded. Sara told how her mother had become angry with her and screamed at her, 'Why don't you just stop being schizophrenic?'

'I just wanted to die; that's why I started the fire,' Sara said in a barely audible voice.

She didn't think about the danger. Sam's willingness to forgive her in spite of this error in judgment made it safe for Sara to share her heart with the group.

It is the 'Sams' of this world who make us a community because of their forgiveness and compassion. For as St Francis of Assisi once said, 'It is in pardoning that we are pardoned.'[9]

ᗋ

# The Gift of Flight

*As each one has received a gift, minister it
to one another, as good stewards of the
manifold grace of God.*
*1 Peter 4:10 NKJV*

They call their flights 'missions'.

On any given day, the volunteers of
AirLifeLine, an American national non-
profit-making organization of recreational
pilots, can be called into action to provide
needy patients with transportation to distant hospitals for lifesaving surgeries and
medical treatments. Without their assis-
tance, many of the recipients, financially
devastated by catastrophic illness, could not
afford the airfare to reach their medical
centres as quickly as needed.

You might not recognize these angels
immediately. With members in all fifty
states, the more than 800 AirLifeLine rep-
resentatives come from every possible
profession and walk of life.

But they share an irrepressible enthusiasm for flying and a desire to give something to their communities. These weekend pilots, always on the look-out for an opportunity to fly somewhere, are happy to donate their time, skills and use of their aircraft to help those in need.

Their passengers are every bit as varied. The case could be a child in need of a kidney transplant or a cancer patient flying to a faraway research centre for experimental treatment.

For Houston pilot Jed Goodall, 'Every mission I fly is heartwarming. I just thank the good Lord that I can afford to fly an airplane. You get so much back yourself from doing this.'[10]

What could be more rewarding than to do something you love and help others at the same time? The Lord's gifts to us are bountiful, but they are multiplied when we take a talent He has given us and spread it around.

## *Feel the Power!*

> *But the fruit of the Spirit is love, joy, peace,*
> *patience, kindness, goodness, faithfulness,*
> *gentleness, self-control.*
> *Galatians 5:22,23 NASB*

Pope John XXIII was once quoted as saying, 'It often happens that I wake at night and begin to think about a serious problem and decide I must tell the Pope about it. Then I wake up completely and remember that I *am* the Pope.'

How often we imagine that the solution to our problems, the cure for our ailments or the guarantee for our happiness lies with someone or something outside ourselves. But do we really have so little power?

Martha Washington thought otherwise, stating, 'I have learned from experience that the greater part of our happiness or misery depends on our dispositions and not on our circumstances. We carry the seeds with us in our minds wherever we go.'

Just think about it. How dramatically would your life be changed if you knew you had the seeds to your happiness waiting inside, longing to blossom whenever you would allow it? From Mother Teresa, in her book, *A Gift to God*, we can learn how to let those seeds spring to life.

*We all long for Heaven where God is but we have it in our power to be in Heaven with Him right now — to be happy with Him at this very moment. But being happy with Him now means:*
*— loving as He loves,*
*— helping as He helps,*
*— giving as He gives,*
*— serving as He serves,*
*— rescuing as He rescues,*
*— being with Him for all the twenty-four hours,*
*— touching Him in His distressing disguise.*

ɶ

# The Lord Directs My Steps

*The mind of man plans his way,*
*but the LORD directs his steps.*
Proverbs 16:9 NASB

The birthday party was going well and the thirteen-year-old girl was thrilled that all of her friends could be there to celebrate with her. Each present was 'just what she wanted'. The last game to be played was Pin The Tail On The Donkey, and everyone was especially excited because the winner would receive a £10 gift token. When the birthday girl had her turn, she lost her footing and stumbled on top of several of her friends.

It was very funny, but the girl wasn't able to get her position right after that and she continued to try to pin the tail everywhere except near the game's paper donkey. When the scarf was removed from her eyes and she saw how far she was from where she needed to be, she said, 'I certainly needed someone to direct my steps.'

God has promised to direct our steps if we will allow Him to do so. The plan for our lives was laid before the beginning of time. Each morning we can go to the Lord and have a fresh look at the direction He would have us go that day.

Are you faced with a major decision? Do you need direction and guidance? Throughout Scripture there are promises that God will show us the right path. We do not have to stumble or grope around blindfolded. Our Heavenly Father is eager to give us wisdom. All we need to do is ask, and He will direct every step we take.

# *The First Valentine*

*We love, because He first loved us.*
*1 John 4:19 NASB*

$\mathcal{M}$ost people would be surprised to learn
that Valentine's Day was not intended to
celebrate romance with gifts of flowers and
chocolate. It was a day to honour a different
kind of love.

Valentine was a Christian priest near
Rome in a period when Christians were
punished for rejecting the Roman gods.

During this persecution, legends say that
Valentine assisted Christians in escaping
from prison. He was discovered, arrested
and sent for trial, where he was asked if he
believed in the Romans' gods. He called
their gods false. He continued to say that
the only true God was He whom Jesus
called 'Father'.

Valentine was imprisoned, but it did not
stop him from continuing his ministry.
Even the prison guards began to listen to

his witness. One was the adoptive father of a blind girl, whom the priest befriended as she waited at the jail while her father worked

When the Roman emperor heard of Valentine's persistent worship of his God, he ordered his execution. In the days before his death, Valentine offered to pray for the jailer's blind daughter and her sight was miraculously restored when he died. As a result, the jailer's entire family – forty-six people – came to believe in the one God and were baptized.

St Valentine knew every step of the way that his activities would endanger his life. But he continued because he loved God and his fellow man. It was a love that deserves to be honoured and modelled every day of the year.

CR

# Obedience and Peaceful Abiding

*Abide in Me, and I in you.*
*John 15:4 NASB*

While on safari, a missionary family stopped for lunch. The children were playing under a tree a distance away from their parents and the other adults on the team. Suddenly the father of one child jumped up and yelled to his son, 'Drop down!' and the son did so instantly. Others in the group were shocked to learn that a poisonous snake was slithering down the tree ready to strike the child. It would have meant certain death if the snake had bitten him. Only the father had seen the snake.

Amazement was expressed over the instant response of the child to his father's command. The father explained the abiding love he and his son enjoyed had developed from the trust they had in each other. The boy did not question when his dad gave the command; he trusted him and responded accordingly. The missionary father also expected his son to respond to his command.

The peaceful rest that both of them were able to enjoy later that day was evidence of the abiding rest that God has for each of us as we learn to trust Him. Are you abiding in Christ?

God wants to abide in us and He wants us to abide in Him. Abiding comes more easily for some than others. It is not always easy to know what God has planned for us, but we can be assured that whatever it is, He is ready to equip us with what we need to endure and hold on to that place for as long as He wants us there. Abiding starts with trust and ends with complete rest.

CR

## *What's the Problem?*

*I can do all things through Christ who
strengthens me.*
*Philippians 4:13 NKJV*

$\mathcal{E}$ver had a difficulty that gives you '2:00
am wake-up calls'? It could be a project at
work, a committee you've suddenly ended
up chairing, or simply trying to figure out
how to get everything done with only two
hands. Whatever the issue, it ruins your
sleep and saps your energy for the day that
is looming.

The developer of a popular series of business training films describes the phenomenon
of discovering your problem-solving skills
are going nowhere:

*You start thinking, I'm uncomfortable. I'm
anxious. I can't do this. I should never have started to try. I'm not creative. I was never creative in
school. I'm a complete failure. I'm going to be
fired, and that means my spouse will leave me and*

*– in other words, you start enjoying a real, good, old-fashioned panic attack.*[11]

Problems can feel ten times as large in the middle of the night. But in reality – and by daylight – solutions might not be as distant as they seem.

Inventor Charles Kettering had a unique problem-solving method. He would divide each problem into the smallest possible pieces, then research the pieces to determine which ones had already been solved. He often found that what looked like a huge problem was already 98 per cent solved by others. Then he tackled what was left.

In bite-sized pieces, problems become more manageable. Remember that, with God, all things are possible. He can give us peace in our darkest nights, and bring wisdom with the morning.

☙

# I Am Father

*I will be careful to lead a blameless life.*
*Psalm 101:2*

As he watched his young son sleep peacefully, Tom thought to himself: *I really am a father*. Since his son was nearly nine years old, the idea of his being a father was nothing new. What was new was his comprehension of all that it means to be a father. The revelation came slowly, but once Tom was conscious of it, he could not get it out of his mind, and in thinking of what a father really is, he could not help but think of his own childhood.

He remembered his father leaning over the old 1957 Chevy pickup truck working far into the night to rebuild the engine. Dad had already put in a full day's work; yet the truck engine needed to be rebuilt and there was no one else to do it.

A second scene played across Tom's mind, and he saw his father sitting at the table eating a late dinner alone. It was close to 10 pm, and he had finally arrived home from his fourteen-hour working day.

He recalled seeing his father at a church workday mowing the grass, trimming the hedges and weeding the flower beds.

More than anything else, his father epitomized the word *responsible* and, for Tom, the knowledge that his own children are now looking to him to be an example just as he looked to his father was quite humbling.

As Tom gently closed the bedroom door, the words of Thomas Morell came to mind. 'The first great gift we can bestow on others is a good example.' Like Tom and his father, we can give the gift of a good example to our children each and every day.

ജ

## *Like a Newborn Babe*

*I will give you a new heart and put a new spirit within you; I will take the heart of stone out of your flesh and give you a heart of flesh.*
*Ezekiel 36:26 NKJV*

In 1994, Jim Gleason underwent a life-saving heart transplant at the age of fifty-one. After one of the most extreme surgeries imaginable, many asked how it felt to live with a new heart. His analogy was '. . . like being born again, but with fifty years of memories and experiences built in . . .'

He tells of coming home just ten days after his transplant. He wanted to go for a short walk around the garden. Accompanied by his daughter, he gazed in wonder at the green grass after weeks of hospital-room walls.

*I stopped walking. 'Look at that!' I exclaimed to Mary. I was pointing to our small* maple tree, so vibrant with the colors of that crisp, clear fall day. Then I spied a grasshopper and, like the young child, exclaimed in glee, 'Look at that! A grasshopper!!'

Her response, in disbelief at my reaction, was an almost sarcastic, 'Well, if that's exciting, look here – a lady bug!'

After four years with his new heart, Jim still cherishes life's simple pleasures. And when is the danger of losing that gift greatest? 'As friends and family wish you would return to being "normal",' he reflects. 'I struggle to never become "normal" in that sense again.'[12]

With God's help, we too can walk in newness of life – no surgery required. Give thanks that we don't have to be 'normal'.

⟨℞⟩

## Say That Again?

*So shall My word be that goes forth from My
mouth; it shall not return to Me void, but it shall
accomplish what I please, and it shall prosper in the
thing for which I sent it.*
Isaiah 55:11 NKJV

In 1954, Sylvia Wright wrote a column
for *The Atlantic* in which she coined the
term 'mondegreen', her code word for misheard lyrics. She recounted hearing for the
first time the Scottish folk song, 'The
Bonny Earl of Morray',

*Ye highlands, and ye lowlands,
Oh! whair hae ye been?
They hae slaine the Earl of Murray,
And layd him on the green.*

She misheard the last line as 'and Lady
Mondegreen'. It saddened her immensely
that both the Earl and the Lady had died.
Of course, she was later chagrined to learn

that those were not the lyrics at all. But they made so much sense at the time.

Since then, mondegreen collectors have been on the lookout for newer and more comical misunderstandings. For example:

In 'America the Beautiful', one young patriot heard 'Oh beautiful, for spacious skies . . .' as 'Oh beautiful, for spaceship guys . . .'

Another considered 'Away in a Manger' a little unsettling as he sang, 'the cattle are blowing the baby away . . .'

Then there was the Mickey Mouse Club fan who, when the cast sang 'Forever hold your banners high . . .' thought they were encouraging her to 'Forever hold your Pampers high!'[13]

It's no wonder that, with all our earthly static and clamour, we sometimes think we're singing the right words when we're not. But if we begin each day in quiet conversation with God, His word comes through loud and clear. There can be no misunderstanding God's lyrics.

CR

## Double Blessing

*And in your godliness, brotherly kindness,*
*and in your brotherly kindness, love.*
*2 Peter 1:7 NASB*

British statesman and financier Cecil Rhodes whose fortune, acquired from diamond mining in Africa, endowed the world-famous Rhodes Scholarships, was known as a stickler for correct dress – but not at the expense of someone else's feelings.

Once it was told that Rhodes invited a young man to an elegant dinner at his home. The guest had to travel a great distance by train and arrived in town only in time to go directly to Rhodes' home in his travel-stained clothes. Once there, he was distressed to find that dinner was ready to be served and the other guests were gathered in their finest evening clothes. But Rhodes was nowhere to be seen. Moments later, he appeared in a shabby old blue suit. The young man later learned that his host had been dressed in evening clothes, but put on the old suit when he heard of his guest's embarrassment.[14]

Rabbi Samuel Holdenson captured the spirit behind Rhodes' gesture, saying:

*Kindness is the inability to remain at ease in the presence of another person who is ill at ease, the inability to remain comfortable in the presence of another who is uncomfortable, the inability to have peace of mind when one's neighbor is troubled.*

The simplest act of kindness not only affects the receiver in profound ways, but brings blessings to the giver as well. It makes us feel good to make others feel good. So do something nice for yourself today – commit a random act of kindness!

ॐ

# Night Driving

*Your word is a lamp to my feet and a light
to my path.*
*Psalm 119:105 NRSV*

$\mathscr{A}$ woman confessed to a friend her confusion and hesitance about an important life
decision she was facing. She professed to
believe in God, but could not bring herself
to rely on her faith to help choose her path.

'How can I know I'm doing the right
thing?' she asked. 'How can I possibly
believe my decision will be right when I
can't even see tomorrow?'

Her friend thought a moment and finally
said, 'Here's how I look at it. You know
when you're driving down a dark country
road with no streetlights to give you any
notion of where you are? It's a little scary.
But you rely on headlights. Now, those
headlights may only show you ten yards of
road in front of you, but you see where to
go for that little stretch. And as you travel

that ten-yard stretch of road, the headlights
show you ten more yards, and ten more,
until eventually you reach your destination
safe and sound.

'That's how I feel about living by faith. I
may not be able to see tomorrow, next
week or next year, but I know that God
will give me the light to find my way when
I need it.'

*When you come to the edge
of all the light you know
and are about to step off
into the darkness of the unknown,
faith is knowing one of two things will happen:
There will be something solid to stand on,
or you will be taught how to fly.*
— Barbara J. Winter

## But When?

*Wait on the LORD; be of good courage,*
*and He shall strengthen your heart.*
*Psalm 27:14 NKJV*

We have often smiled knowingly at that kitchen-magnet quip, 'Lord, give me patience, and give it to me now!' And why not? Our society expects immediate accomplishment in almost everything we do – from microwave meals in minutes to global communication in seconds.

It seems, whatever the problem, there should be a button, switch or pill to deliver fast results. Which makes it all the more difficult to accept that, like it or not, spiritual growth takes time.

In a garden, all seedlings have average schedules of development. But as human beings with unique histories and needs, we can't rely on averages to determine when we might take that next step in our walk with God.

It's tempting, when faced with a flaw of the spirit or other growth issue, to pray for and expect immediate change. Sometimes it happens. But how lost and confused we feel if our prayers don't bring the instant relief we seek.

During such times, it's good to remember that all facets of our nature — whether traits we love about ourselves or those we want to improve — are part of our God-created being. Even our less-than-desirable parts are there for a reason and contain His lessons for us.

When change seems to come slowly, don't give up hope. Consider that the timetable for your growth is in the Lord's hands. Continue your daily communion with God and trust your spirit to be healed *in His time.*

∞

# Hearing with the Heart

*Because thine heart was tender.*
*2 Kings 22:19 KJV*

'We've wasted my whole Saturday,'
moaned John as his father gently woke
him.

The plaintive, anguished tone of his voice
created an instant reaction in his father and
a flash of anger surged upwards. It had
been a very long day of painting and hang-
ing wallpaper in Mum's new office and
Dad was tired. John had worked hard earlier in the day, but as the novelty wore off
he became bored and eventually fell asleep
on a couch in an adjacent office. Now his
Dad, Richard, was waking him so that they
could head home.

Before Richard could voice the quick
retort that formed in his mind, something
caused him to pause. In a flash, he saw the
Saturday spent working in Mum's new
office from an eight-year-old's point of view.

With newfound compassion he responded to his son, 'John, I know that Saturday is just about the most important day of the week when you're eight. I appreciate so much your willingness to give up your Saturday to help us get Mum's office decorated. It has been a very long day and I bet that you're tired too. But, I would like to show you how much I appreciate your support by stopping by the video store on the way home so that you can choose a film to rent. What do you say?'

In response to Dad's caring attitude, John's anguish and despair turned to pride and he quietly said, 'You're welcome, Dad. I would like that.'

Sometimes, when we listen with our heart and not our ears, love wins and relationships flourish. For, as Johann Wolfgang Von Goethe says, 'Correction does much, but encouragement does more.'

☙

## *Morning Thirst*

*My soul thirsts for God, for the living God.*
*Psalm 42:2 NASB*

The need for a refreshing drink when we first wake in the morning is often so strong that we find ourselves anticipating the taste before we ever get a glass in our hands. That thirst is a driving force that nothing else will satisfy.

There is another thirst that needs to be quenched when we first wake up. A thirst we often ignore until it is so great, that everything else in our lives – relationships, our growth as a child of God, our joy, our peace – begins to wither.

Patti did not have running water inside her home when she was a child. Not since then has she known that same level of satisfaction a morning drink of water can give. This was especially true if the water in the house ran out during the night when it was too cold or too stormy for anyone to make a trip to the source outside. Sometimes it was a long, long wait for morning.

There is a source of living water that is available to us any time of the day or night. It never runs out, it never gets contaminated, it never freezes over, and it is always as refreshing throughout the day as it was with the first sip in the morning.

Renowned missionary Hudson Taylor said, 'There is a living God, He has spoken in the Bible and He means what He says and He will do all that He has promised.' He has promised to quench our thirst in such a way that we will never be thirsty again!

Are you anticipating a drink from God's cup of refreshing living water in the morning? God gives you permission to start sipping right now. *Bon appetit!*

# *The Face of God*

*No man has beheld God at any time; if we love one
another, God abides in us, and His love
is perfected in us.*
*1 John 4:12 NASB*

Dutch psychologist and theologian
Henri Nouwen was known for his determination to break down barriers, whether
between Catholic and Protestant or therapist and patient. He spent most of his life
pursuing a high-pressure career as a
sought-after speaker and author.

But years of travel and dozens of books
took such a toll on his health and spirit that
he eventually retreated to Toronto, Canada,
to become priest-in-residence at Daybreak,
a home for the severely disabled.

Nouwen lived a quiet life at Daybreak,
residing in a small, simple room and minis-
tering to the patients there. He had a special relationship with a resident named
Adam, a profoundly retarded young man

unable to walk, talk or care for himself.
Nouwen devoted nearly two hours every
day to caring for Adam – bathing, shaving,
combing his hair, feeding him.

To onlookers, it seemed a great burden
on the priest to spend so many hours on
such menial duties. But when asked why he
spent his time in this way, Nouwen insisted
that it was he who benefited from the relationship. He described how the process of
learning to love Adam, with all of his inca-
pacities, taught him what it must be like for
God to love us, even with all our frailties.

Ultimately, Henri Nouwen concluded
that 'the goal of education and formation
for the ministry is continually to recognize
the Lord's voice, His face, and His touch in
every person we meet'.[15]

Have you seen the Lord's face lately?

CR

# *What Do You Think?*

*The eyes of the LORD preserve knowledge.*
*Proverbs 22:12 KJV*

'Dad, have you heard of this book?' Cindy asked, showing him a copy of a highly controversial work. Rev Bill looked up from his desk to respond to his sixteen-year-old daughter.

'Sure, I have, why do you ask?' he replied.

In fact, he knew a great deal about the book. It had recently been made into a film that was causing quite a stir in the Christian community, and many pastors and church members were so upset that they had even picketed the cinemas where the film was showing.

'I was just wondering if it is a good book,' Cindy answered.

'Why don't you read it for yourself and then we will talk about it together?'

In that moment, Bill demonstrated a

remarkable faith in his daughter, his own parenting and his God. By inviting her to read and discuss this book, he was saying that he trusted Cindy to think for herself. Beyond his faith in her, he modelled his faith in God by trusting that her faith would provide guidance as she made decisions.

The single greatest challenge we face as parents is that of letting go of our children the right way and at the right time. Nowhere is this faith challenged more than in the arena of controversial ideas. Yet, we can have confidence that what we have taught them will keep them, for Scripture says, *'Train a child in the way he should go, and when he is old he will not turn from it'* (Proverbs 22:6).

Bill could trust Cindy because he knew that her entire life had been one characterized by learning the Word of God, and now it was time to put that learning to the test.

ℭℜ

# A Work in Progress

*For we are His workmanship, created in Christ
Jesus for good works, which God prepared before-
hand that we should walk in them.*
*Ephesians 2:10 NKJV*

*M*any centuries ago, a young Greek
artist named Timanthes studied under a
respected tutor. After several years of
effort, Timanthes painted an exquisite work
of art. Unfortunately, he was so taken with
his painting that he spent days gazing at it.

One morning, he arrived to find his work
blotted out with paint. His teacher admitted
destroying the painting, saying, 'I did it for
your own good. That painting was retard-
ing your progress. Start again and see if
you can do better.' Timanthes took his
teacher's advice and produced *Sacrifice of
Iphigenia*, now regarded as one of the finest
paintings of antiquity.[16]

Timanthes' teacher knew what many
great artists know – we should never con-

sider ourselves truly finished with our
work.

When the legendary Pablo Casals
reached his ninety-fifth year, a reporter
asked, 'Mr Casals, you are ninety-five and
the greatest cellist who ever lived. Why do
you still practise six hours a day?' And
Casals answered, 'Because I think I'm making progress.'

Maya Angelou applies that same logic to
daily life. In her book, *Wouldn't Take Nothin'
for My Journey Now*, she writes: 'Many
things continue to amaze me, even well into
the sixth decade of my life. I'm startled or
taken aback when people walk up to me
and tell me they are Christians. My first
response is the question "Already?" It
seems to me a lifelong endeavor to try to
live the life of a Christian . . .'[17]

How exciting it is to be a work in
progress. With God's help, our possibilities
are limitless!

## Touching Life

*Preserve my life according to your love.*
*Psalm 119:88*

The sounds of the delivery room receded to a quiet murmur of post-delivery activities and near-whispered comments between the parents. The father, gowned, with a hair net and masked face, leaned forward, touching their child who was cuddled to the mother. She looked down on the baby who was scowling, her eyes tightly shut. With a sense of awe, the mother stretched forth one finger to gently smooth the child's wrinkled forehead. The need to touch her daughter was urgent, yet she was careful.

Developmental psychologists who have examined the process of childbirth and witnessed thousands of deliveries inform us that the need to gently touch one's newborn is a near-universal impulse crossing all cultural boundaries. Obviously, we have been created with an innate need to physically connect with our offspring.

In this sense we are very much like God.

In *The Creation of Adam*, one of Michaelangelo's famous frescoes that decorate the ceiling of the Sistine Chapel, he portrays the hand of Adam outstretched with a finger pointed. Opposite to it you see the hand of God in a similar pose reaching towards man. The two fingertips are nearly touching. No image more clearly reveals the Father's heart. He is ever-reaching out His hand to touch, with gentleness and love, those who are created in His own image.

Mothers and God share a common bond then, do they not? Both possess a deep reverence for the life that they have brought into the world. Both yearn to touch those made in their image.

CR

## Doing Right

*'This is My beloved Son, in whom I am well pleased.'*
*Matthew 3:17 NKJV*

'*I* waited and waited, and Morgan never came back.' Will's eyes filled to the brim and then tears overflowed to run down his cheeks as he sobbed his story to his father. He was a very grown-up four-year-old, and he did not want to cry, but he couldn't help it.

'It's OK to cry, Will,' his father responded. 'Tell me what happened.'

With a big sniffle, Will continued, 'I know that I'm not supposed to go past the end of the building. Morgan was playing with me. He said that he wanted to go to the pool and that he would be right back. I waited and waited, but he never came back to play with me.'

With a tug at his heart, Will's father knelt and gathered him into his arms. As Will melted against his chest, his crying eased and his father said, 'Will, I am so proud of you. When you obey me when we are together it makes me happy. But, nothing compares to how good you make me feel when you do the right thing even when I am not around. Thank you. I love you very much, my little man.'

The tears soon dried and Will went on about his business of playing. His wounded heart had been tended to, and things were better because of the love and assurance he received from his father. In fact, he beamed with happiness when his father bragged about him.

God the Father is like that too, you know. He is touched by the pain His children cause one another, and His heart is filled with joy when we obey simply because it is the right thing to do.

CR

# Fine China

*Behold, like the clay in the potter's hand,*
*so are you in My hand, O house of Israel.*
Jeremiah 18:6 NASB

Antique hunting one day, a collector
noticed a lovely teacup and saucer. The delicate set stood out from the other china
pieces in the display. She picked up the cup
and examined it carefully. Discovering a
small imperfection on the bottom, she lovingly held it in her hands as she thought
about what might have caused the cup's
flaw.

A few years earlier while visiting a pot-
tery shop, she had watched as the potter
chose a lump of clay to work and began to
punch and slam it over and over again until
it was just right. He shaped it, painted it
and fired it into a beautiful piece of earth-
enware that would be looked upon admir-
ingly and be a serviceable item as well.

The clay, useless in its original form, had

become beautiful, strong and useful in the potter's hands. The woman thought of her own life with all its flaws, yet Jesus was willing to sacrifice Himself so that she could have a good life with Him. Many lumpy places had existed in her heart prior to her salvation, but Jesus Christ, the Master Craftsman, began His work of shaping and moulding, lovingly concentrating on even the finest details. This human vessel was then made fit for His service as He gently filled it to overflowing with the refining work of the Holy Spirit.

As she stepped up to the counter to purchase the cup and saucer she whispered a prayer. 'Lord, help me to never forget what You saved me from, the price You paid, and the hope I have of one day being in heaven's display as a fine piece worthy of You.'

*CR*

## Sunrise

*The sunrise from on high shall visit us.*
*Luke 1:78 NASB*

Sunrise, shining its beams through the window on a cold winter's morning, is a welcome sight. Even if the air outside is icy cold, sunrise gives the illusion of warmth. With the rising sun, the city opens its shutters and makes preparations for the day; in the country, the farm animals are let out to pasture. Kids are off to school, adults are on their way to work, and each has a different perspective of the sunrise.

Sunrise happens whether we see it or not. Clouds may cover the sky so totally that we can't experience the beauty of the sunbeams making their way to the earth. No matter what the climate, the sun still rises in the eastern horizon and sets over the west. Sunrise is set by God's clock, and it is ours to enjoy in the early mornings when we can see it clearly. It is just as much there for us to enjoy when the cloud shadows cover it. We can trust it to be there – even though it may be hidden for a while.

We can also trust God to be there every morning because He is the one, irrefutable reality in this life, and He remains constant and true!

*Life is a mixture of sunshine and rain,*
*Laughter and teardrops, pleasure and pain –*
*Low tides and high tides, mountains and plains,*
*Triumphs, defeats and losses and gains.*
*But there never was a cloud*
*That the Son didn't shine through*
*And there's nothing that's impossible*
*For Jesus Christ to do!*
*– Helen Steiner Rice*

## New Day

*A faithful man will be richly blessed.*
*Proverbs 28:20*

'Yesterday is gone and you cannot do anything about what happened then!'

'Move on!'

'Don't cry over spilt milk!'

All of the old clichés and sayings came to his mind as he walked from the courtroom. Jim's marriage was finished. He had failed in his marriage. He was the first person in his family to divorce, and the reality of it was crushing.

*What must my family really think of me?* he wondered.

A couple of months later, a snowy winter evening provided the answer. Jim had travelled from his home in southern Texas to visit his brother for Christmas in a small town high in the Colorado Rockies. It was already dark when the bus pulled into the car park of the service station.

Huge snowflakes gently fell, and everything was covered in snow. Jim was tired and feeling anxious as he stepped down from the bus. Suddenly, his older brother Steve was there, and Jim was engulfed in the bear hug to end all bear hugs. As Jim looked up, he saw their father standing at the edge of the car park with a smile on his face. Their welcome told him he was loved.

Their simple message had a profound impact on Jim's life. It did not magically take all his pain away, but with time he was able to gain strength and encouragement whenever he remembered that powerful message of love and acceptance sent through a hug on a snowy winter's evening.

No matter what we have done, we are worthy and welcome in God's kingdom and each day is indeed a new day. Henry Wadsworth Longfellow penned this truth: 'The lowest ebb is the turn of the tide.'

## *Everyone's a Critic*

*Therefore, let those also who suffer according to
the will of God entrust their souls to a faithful
Creator in doing what is right.*
*1 Peter 4:19 NASB*

Winston Churchill exemplified integrity
and respect in the face of opposition.
During his last year in office, he attended
an official ceremony. Several rows behind
him two gentlemen began whispering,
'That's Winston Churchill. They say he is
getting senile. They say he should step
aside and leave the running of the nation to
more dynamic and capable men.'

When the ceremony ended, Churchill
turned to the men and said, 'Gentlemen,
they also say he is deaf!'[18]

Most people find it difficult to ignore the
brunt of public opinion. It's easier to do
things they don't want to do, or not do
what they feel is right, rather than stand up
for their own desires and convictions. One

writer called it 'worshipping the god of other people's opinion'.

In the words of Ralph Waldo Emerson:

*Whatever you do, you need courage. Whatever course you decide upon, there is always someone to tell you you are wrong. There are always difficulties arising that tempt you to believe that your critics are right. To map out a course of action and follow it to an end requires some of the same courage that a soldier needs. Peace has its victories, but it takes brave people to win them.*

Ignoring the god of other people's opinion requires strength and focus. Fortunately, we know the God who can grant us that strength and stand with us as we pursue the paths we feel are right. His opinion is the only one that counts.

**CR**

## *Sensitivity*

> *'Do not touch My anointed ones.'*
> *Psalm 105:15 NASB*

On the Big Island of Hawaii grows a delicate little plant called Sensitivity, a member of the Mimosa family. Its name is derived from the movement it makes when anything, including a change in the wind, comes near or across it. This minute, spiny stemmed tropical American plant, grows close to the ground. Unless you are directly upon it, you can't distinguish it from grass or weeds in the same area and it can easily be crushed underfoot.

As the sun rises in the South Pacific, the tiny Sensitivity plant opens itself as wide as it can and reaches up towards the warmth of the early morning sunbeams shining down from heaven. This wee drooping plant has a built-in mechanism that causes it to quickly fold itself over and withdraw from anything that might cause it harm.

However, Sensitivity can't distinguish between a lawn mower rolling towards it to cut it down from the man coming by to make certain it is protected.

Each of us has a built-in need to protect ourselves from danger and those who would harm us. God gave us His Word as a manual to equip us to be aware of the ways of the enemy and to prepare us to know how to protect ourselves.

We can reach up every morning, even when it's raining or snowing, and receive His warmth, His love, His protection and His anointing for the day ahead of us. God has blessed us with His sensitivity, but we must be alert by using the tools He has provided for us.

CR

# *Try, Try Again*

*Though he stumble, he will not fall.*
*Psalm 37:24*

$\mathcal{T}$he election results were discouraging
for Bob. He had been absolutely certain
that he would be elected State President of
the National Community College Honor
Society. His college's chapter had success-
fully been elected president at the state con-
vention and he had played a pivotal role in
the campaign. So, when they met to select
one of their members to hold the office he
believed it would be him. He was wrong.

'Well,' he reasoned, 'there is still the
presidency of the local college chapter. I am
sure that I will win that.'

He was not elected to this office either.
Instead, he was elected chapter vice-presi-
dent. Though disappointed, he did not give
up his dream. And, when the elected
chapter president withdrew from college
Bob became the local president. The story

does not end there though.

During the next year, Bob asked his chapter members if they would support him in a bid for National President of the entire Honor Society. The chapter enthusiastically agreed and the next April he was elected National President of the Community College Honor Society. He had triumphed over thirteen other candidates.

The lesson he learned from this experience is that you never achieve your goals unless you set them high enough. In other words, for Bob it became essential that he raise his expectations for himself when he did not achieve the goal he had set. Originally, he would have been delighted to serve as a State President. Eventually, he was honoured to serve as the National President.

He is a living example of Calvin Coolidge's words, 'Nothing in the world can take the place of persistence. Persistence and determination alone are omnipotent.'

## *Morning Drive*

*This is the day the LORD has made;*
*we will rejoice and be glad in it.*
*Psalm 118:24 NKJV*

$\mathcal{J}$udy could take the motorway to work each morning and arrive instantly, nerves revved, almost before she is awake. But motorways are ugly. Instead she takes the scenic route around several local lakes and starts her day with mental pictures of sunrises, flowers and people in various states of running and walking.

Affluence and architecture notwithstanding, she feels that nature is the attraction – a chance for a city slicker to enjoy a little tranquillity. The slower pace gives her the occasion to see a small troop of deer or watch the ducks and geese depart for the winter and return for their spring nesting activities. She recognizes and studies the walkers and joggers who are out regularly at the crack of dawn.

'I don't know if I have a better workday because I sneak up on the job rather than race to it,' she muses. 'On some mornings, I don't see one thing that nature has to offer because the day ahead refuses to wait for me to get there, and I spend the entire ride making lists of things to do in my head. But I do know that when I take the time to glance at the roses along the way, I feel more fortified, just like our mothers wanted us to be with a hearty breakfast, mittens, and hats.'[19]

Taking a few moments to thank God for the glories of creation will make any day start on a better note!

☙

# The Master

*The LORD your God in your midst, the Mighty One,
will save; He will rejoice over you with gladness,
He will quiet you with His love, He will rejoice
over you with singing.*
Zephaniah 3:17 NKJV

The story is told of a concert appearance by the brilliant Polish composer and pianist Ignace Jan Paderewski. The event was staged in a great American music hall, where the artist was to perform for the social elite of the city.

Waiting in the audience for the concert to begin was a woman and her young son. After sitting for longer than his patience could stand, the youngster slipped away from his mother. He was fascinated by the beautiful Steinway piano awaiting the performance and made his way towards it. Before anyone knew what was happening, he had crept onto the stage and climbed up on the piano stool to play a round of

'Chopsticks'.

The audience was horrified. What would the great Paderewski think? The murmurs quickly erupted into a roar of disapproval as the crowd demanded that the child be removed immediately.

Backstage, Paderewski heard the disruption and, discerning the cause, raced out to join the child at the piano. He reached around him from behind and improvised his own countermelody to his young guest's 'Chopsticks'. As the impromptu duet continued, the master whispered in the child's ear, 'Keep going. Don't quit, son . . . don't stop . . . don't stop.'[20]

We may never play alongside a master pianist, but every day in our lives can be a duet with the Master. What joy it is to feel His love wrapped around us as He whispers, 'Keep going . . . don't stop . . . I am with you.'

CR

## Morning Woods

*And the peace of God, which transcends
all understanding, will guard your hearts.*
*Philippians 4:7*

*I*t's quiet and still as the solitary hunter,
bundled up and in camouflage hunting
gear, waits for daylight. Sunrise is still a
way off and the East Texas woods are just
beginning to stir with life. The air is cold;
bare branches click against one another. At
the edge of the clearing, waist-high sedge
grass stirs in the breeze. To the east, the
sky lightens, and one can just begin to
make out individual trees among the forest.

Slowly, minutes pass. Squirrels chatter
and bark at one another. An armadillo wad-
dles by, nuzzling the fallen leaves aside in
search of a breakfast of grubs, and a small
rabbit, nose and whiskers twitching a mile
a minute, carefully moves down towards a
small pool of water. It's so still you can
hear the soft thump of its large feet as they
hit the moist earth.

Tall pines stand out boldly against the brightening sky. Small sparrows and finches dart from tree to tree; large black crows screech a harsh greeting to the new day; and somewhere in the distance, a hoot owl bids goodbye to the parting darkness. Into this rich tableau a large grey timber wolf trots into view following a game trail, wasting no time as it moves quickly down the path and then vanishes into the underbrush.

The hunter, sitting on the tree-stand for some hours by now, without ever lifting his rifle, feels that this has been the finest time he has ever experienced in the woods. He discovered a peace rarely found in today's fast-paced world. For him, this quiet December morning brought new meaning to the verse, *'Be still, and know that I am God'* (Psalm 46:10 KJV).

❦

## Time for a Change

*Now faith is the assurance of things hoped for,*
*the conviction of things not seen.*
*Hebrews 11:1 NASB*

Skier Jean-Claude Killy was ready to
do whatever it took – no matter how hard
the work – to be the best when he made the
French national team in the early 1960s.
But after months of gruelling practice, he
recognized that his competitors were put-
ting in just as much effort in the same kind
of training. It was then he decided to go a
step further and find different ways to ski
faster rather than just working harder.

He started testing every part of his racing
technique, such as altering the accepted leg
positions and using his poles in unorthodox
ways. Soon, his experiments resulted in an
explosive new style that cut his racing
times dramatically. Within a few years,
Killy won virtually every major skiing trophy and three gold medals in the 1968

Winter Olympics.[21]

Killy learned an important lesson in creativity: Innovations don't require genius – just a willingness to question the norms and try something different.

It's been said that one reason people eventually stop growing and learning is they become less willing to risk failure by trying new ideas or experiences. Change can be difficult and uncomfortable. But if our ambitions are only to avoid the discomforts of life, we could soon find we have very little life at all.

God wants us to have the most joyful, fulfilling life possible, and sometimes that requires stepping out into the unknown. Is there a new experience or idea you've been hesitant to pursue? You'll never know until you try.

CR

## Braveheart

*Beloved, you do faithfully whatever you do for the
friends, even though they are strangers to you.*
3 John 5 NRSV

Kevin tells the story of a dear friend
and fellow church member who passed
away after a long life of love and service.

At the funeral, his children stood up one
by one to tell stories about their father, and
soon you noticed a recurring theme: that
his single most outstanding trait was his
willingness to serve others, no matter what
the need. He was one of those people who
was always ready to lend a hand – to run
an errand, do odd jobs, or give someone a
ride home. One of his daughters mentioned
how everywhere he went, he kept a toolbox
and a pair of overalls in the boot of his car,
'just in case somebody needed something
fixed'.

More often than not, when we hear the
word 'courage', we think of heroic acts in

times of crisis. But in our everyday lives, we shouldn't overlook the courageousness of simply being there. Lives are changed when we faithfully provide for our families, care for the elderly or lend an ear to a troubled friend. Persistence in making this world a better place to live – for ourselves and others – is definitely a form of courage.

Albert Schweitzer, the great Christian missionary, doctor and theologian, was once asked in an interview to name the greatest living person. He immediately replied, 'The greatest person in the world is some unknown individual who at this very moment has gone in love to help another.'

As you go about your work today, remember that you could be someone else's hero.

## *Seek and Find*

*I love them that love me; and those
that seek me early shall find me.*
*Proverbs 8:17 KJV*

The parents of a teenager were struggling with constant calls from their child's school, the youth director at church and even other parents in the same community, all complaining about the behaviour of their fifteen-year-old. Distraught and discouraged, the parents rose early one morning and sought the Lord on behalf of their child. Although not in the habit of praying together or for their children prior to this, they found the Lord there for them on that morning and every morning after that. This morning prayer time became the one time they longed for all during the day.

Not only was the habit of praying together started, but reading the Bible together as well. Each day the Lord had many new lessons to teach them. They were learning and growing as individuals and as a couple, and soon they noticed positive changes in their daughter's behaviour as well. Eventually, what the parents had begun as a united effort – to cry out for help to the Lord on their daughter's behalf – was fast becoming a time when the whole family would get together for devotions and worship.

When their daughter saw the transformation in her mother and father, she decided to make some changes in her life, too. Today she is a godly young woman who loves the Lord with all her heart.

When we seek the Lord for a specific need, we find He is ready to meet us for all our needs.

## By Your Fruit

*Love, joy, peace, patience, kindness, goodness, faithfulness, gentleness and self-control. Against such things there is no law.*
Galatians 5:22,23

With these words, Mother Teresa explained a lifetime of service:

*I can love only one person at a time. I can feed only one person at a time. Just one, one, one. So you begin . . . I begin. I picked up one person — maybe if I didn't pick up that one person I wouldn't have picked up 42,000.*[22]

When she died, an entire world mourned.

Sometime before her death, a college professor asked his students to name people they considered truly worthy of the title 'world leader'. Although many different names appeared on the class list, the one name most commonly agreed upon was Mother Teresa.

'She transcends normal love.'

'She has a capacity for giving that makes me ashamed of my own self-centred actions.'

'The most remarkable thing about her is that she never grows tired of her work. She never experiences "burnout" like so many other people. I just hope that I can be as satisfied with my life as she is with hers.'

Although none of the students had ever met her, they acknowledged that Mother Teresa had a profound impact on each of their lives. How? By her love. She welcomed the opportunity to fulfil her duties. Can we do any less?

Next time you have a chance to be kind remember her words: 'It is not how much we do but how much love we put in the doing.'[23] Isn't it exciting to know that each of us can *put enough love into the doing*, if we so decide, to be a 'Mother Teresa' for at least one other person?

Who knows what would happen if we would all just begin.

## May I Take Your Order?

*Then shall ye call upon me, and ye shall go and
pray unto me, and I will hearken unto you.*
Jeremiah 29:12 KJV

Sometimes, the only solution for a difficult day is nice double-dip ice cream cone –
that is, if you love ice cream. One fan
described a recent trial in ordering her treat
at a drive-through window.

She drove up to the speaker to place her
order. This ice-cream franchise carried too
many flavours to list them all on the menu,
so customers had to ask if a special flavour
was in stock. The attendant answered:

'May I take your order?'

'Do you have butter brickle today?' It
was her favourite since childhood and was
becoming difficult to find.

'No, I'm sorry . . . can we get you anything else?'

Oh, the frustration of drive-through
communication. 'What else do you have?'

she asked.

The attendant paused. 'Well . . . what do you want?'

She couldn't help herself. 'I *want* butter brickle!'

It was useless. But, determined to find that flavour, she drove two miles to the next ice-cream drive-through. She approached the speaker with optimism.

'May I take your order?'

'Yes, do you have butter brickle today?'

After a long pause, the attendant responded, 'Butter brickle *what*?'

It is so disheartening to feel that no one hears our needs. How fortunate that God not only understands our every desire, but knows them even before we do. Philippians 4:6 ASV encourages, '*In nothing be anxious; but in everything by prayer and supplication with thanksgiving let your requests be made known unto God.*' In His care we are assured our needs will be supplied.

 console

## Got Change?

*For God has not given us a spirit of fear, but*
*of power and of love and of a sound mind.*
2 Timothy 1:7 NKJV

A lecturer once told this story of a coun-
selling patient who hated her job and
thought it was ruining her life. But
throughout her therapy she seemed totally
unwilling to improve her situation.

When he suggested she hunt for a new
job, she complained that there were no
decent jobs in her small town.

He asked if she had considered looking
for a job in the next town, fifteen miles
away. She said that she would need a car to
travel that far, and she didn't have one.

When the therapist offered a plan to purchase an inexpensive car, she countered
that it would never work, because 'there's
no place to park in the neighbouring town
anyway'!

It's said that three things in life are certain: death, taxes and change. If you look around, you'll notice that most people can deal with the first two better than change. But without it, we'll never know how wonderful the plans God has for us can be.

Fear of change comes from fear of loss, even if we are losing something that we never liked in the first place. If you are struggling with change in your life today, take a moment to bring your fears to the Lord. With faith in His guidance, change can lead to a blessing!

*Our real blessings often appear to us*
*in the shapes of pains, losses, and*
*disappointments;*
*but let us have patience,*
*and we soon shall see them in their proper figures.*
— Joseph Addison

## Power of Love

*Do not seek revenge or bear a grudge.*
*Leviticus 19:18*

Renowned writer Jack London paints an incredible picture of savagery and hope in his book *White Fang*, the story of a wolf dog who is as an outcast at war with a world where only one law exists: eat or be eaten. 'There was no soil for kindliness and affection to blossom in. The code he learned was to obey the strong and oppress the weak.'[24]

The story is a bold one where the love of one man, Weedon Scott, finally overcomes the fear, hatred and abuse of a lifetime. In fact, London dubs Scott the 'Love Master' because through love and patience he reaches a well deep within White Fang and forges an unshakable bond of love and trust.

In some ways this is a projection of London's own life, though the book had a happier ending than London, who died at the early age of forty after a life characterized by many hard times. He never knew who his father was. He worked at many different jobs, endured time in jail for vagrancy, and saw his fortune evaporate as fast as he made it. Nevertheless, he never gave up hope, and he was always the romanticist at heart.

Commentator Dwight V. Swain states, 'In *White Fang*, clearly London is arguing that love is a major – if not *the* major – civilizing force in a world otherwise ruled by club and fang, brutality and blood.'[25]

Be ever mindful of the power of love, even in today's world, which is sometimes ruled by 'club and fang, brutality and blood'. You will discover ways to be a Weedon Scott in your neighbourhood and community. And, like London, never give up hope or lose faith in the power of love.

CR

## The Value of Disaster

*And not only that, but we also glory in tribulations,*
*knowing that tribulation produces perseverance.*
*Romans 5:3 NKJV*

For ten years Thomas Edison attempted
to invent a storage battery. His efforts
greatly strained his finances, then in
December 1914 nearly brought him to ruin
when a spontaneous combustion broke out
in his film room. Within minutes all the
packing compounds, celluloid for records
and film, and other flammable goods were
ablaze. Though fire departments came from
eight surrounding towns, the intense heat
and low water pressure made attempts to
douse the flames futile. Everything was
destroyed.

While the damage exceeded $2,000,000,
the concrete buildings, thought to be fire-
proof, were insured for barely a tenth of
that amount. The inventor's 24-year-old son
Charles searched frantically for his father,

afraid that his spirit would be broken. Charles finally found him, calmly watching the fire, his face glowing in the reflection, white hair blowing in the wind.

'My heart ached for him,' said Charles. 'He was 67 – no longer a young man – and everything was going up in flames.

'When he saw me, he shouted, "Charles, where's your mother?" When I told him I didn't know, he said, "Find her. Bring her here. She will never see anything like this as long as she lives." '

The next morning, Edison looked at the ruins and said, 'There is great value in disaster. All our mistakes are burned up. Thank God we can start anew.' Three weeks after the fire, Edison managed to deliver the first phonograph.[26]

With each new day, we have the opportunity to start again, to start fresh – no matter what our circumstances. Let the Lord show you how to salvage hope from debris. You never know what joys are ahead.

CR

# *I Know That Voice!*

*The sheep follow him because they know his voice.*
John 10:4 NASB

A young mother had been alone with her preschoolers for a week while her husband was away on a business trip. The fourth day was particularly exasperating. After several bedtime stories, she finally got the energetic children to bed and decided to relax. She had changed into an old tracksuit and shampooed her hair when she heard the children jumping around in their room.

Wrapping a towel around her head, she went to scold them. As she walked out of the children's room, she overheard the littlest one ask, 'Who was that?'

In our busy lives we often overlook God's presence. We can be so out of practice at listening to Him that we fail to recognize His voice and then we miss out on His guidance and grace. Have you ever found yourself asking, 'Who was that?' only later to realize that it was indeed Christ?

When a sheep refuses to follow, the shepherd has no choice but to teach the sheep a lesson for its own protection. The shepherd will break one of its legs and carry the sheep around his neck until its leg heals. The animal becomes so acquainted with his master's voice and ways that it then graciously follows and obeys. Though a difficult lesson, the shepherd saves one who would otherwise be lost.

God wants us to know Him so well that we immediately recognize His voice and obey His commands. There is no better way to know the Master's voice than through an intimate relationship with Him. A perfect time to develop an awareness of the Father's voice is in the early morning when we can quietly sit and listen.

CR

## *Destiny: First Chair or . . .*

*In all labour there is profit.*
*Proverbs 14:23 KJV*

*T*ony's voice was marked by satisfaction as he spoke of his years in the music industry. 'Oh, I could play the trumpet a little bit, and a few other instruments, but as for real talent, I didn't have any. But I do love music and this business.'

Over the past thirty years he had been involved with the publication of music and the production of shows in a variety of capacities. But, according to Tony, the most important decision he ever made occurred when he was a trumpet player in a local orchestra.

'I can remember sitting in the orchestra pit looking up at this young guy who handed some papers to the conductor. They talked for quite a while, and the young guy left.' The young man was a music arranger, and Tony said, 'That changed my life, because I decided right then and there that I wanted to do the same thing.'

Over the next several years, Tony pursued and received his undergraduate degree in music with special emphasis on arrangement. He became a successful professional working for a major music publishing company. Today he serves as a manager and leader in the company. As he nears retirement, Tony obviously loves his chosen profession.

William Jennings Bryan once said, 'Destiny is not a matter of chance, it is a matter of choice; it is not a thing to be waited for; it is a thing to be achieved.'[27]

Are you at a standstill in your work? Does it feel like a dead end? Are you feeling restless? Ask the Lord to show you a better way to share your talents with the world. He will surely open new doors for you.

CR

# Let the River Flow

*But do not forget to do good and to share,
for with such sacrifices God is well pleased.
Hebrews 13:16 NKJV*

The Dead Sea, located between Israel and Jordan, is famous as the lowest point on the surface of the earth. It is also a lively tourist attraction for its healthy spas, where visitors bathe in the salty seawater and flock to purchase cosmetics made from Dead Sea mud.

Have you ever wondered why it is called the Dead Sea? Unlike most large lakes, it has no outlet. The Jordan River flows into the Dead Sea, but nothing flows out. Without sharing what it receives, it dies.

The same is true for people. When we receive gifts of talent, education, financial fortune or other resources, we might think sharing those gifts with others leaves less for us. But when you don't give of yourself to others, a part of you dies.

As Dr David Livingstone once commented:

*People talk of the sacrifice I have made in spending so much of my life in Africa. Can that be called a sacrifice which is simply acknowledging a great debt we owe to our God, which we can never repay? Is that a sacrifice which brings its own reward in healthful activity, the consciousness of doing good, peace of mind, and a bright hope of a glorious destiny? It is emphatically no sacrifice. Rather it is a privilege . . . Of this we ought not to talk, when we remember the great sacrifice which He made Who left His Father's throne on high to give Himself for us.*

May the river of God's love flow through us to everyone we meet.

## *A Reason to Rise*

*Arise, shine, for your light has come,*
*and the glory of the LORD rises upon you.*
*Isaiah 60:1*

While camping deep in the woods, the first sense to attract our attention each morning is . . . smell. The aromatic whiffs of food cooked over an open flame are a wonderful treat to awakening senses. The savory aroma of bacon, sausage and especially a fresh pot of coffee, gently moves through the forest and rests overhead just long enough to rouse the sleeping camper and produce a memory like no other. Years later campers talk about that experience as if they were reliving it, almost capable of smelling the coffee right then. It's a wake-up call campers fondly cherish.

Each of us has moments like these that provide a platform for past memories that are special to us. These classic times of pleasure linger in our minds, much like the

smells of a delicious breakfast on a long ago
camping trip. The first call of the morning
brings us into the new day and helps to set
the pace and tone for the tasks ahead.

Could it be that as followers of Christ,
we experience wake-up calls in our lives
that are for more than just reminiscing?
Our wake-up calls, lessons learned, and
'deserts crossed' with God's help and presence, can turn these experiences into
opportunities that allow God's loving plans
for our lives to shine through us to a lost
and depraved world.

Isaiah shouted, 'Arise, shine!' Share the
joy of knowing Christ with others. There
are many who would otherwise never
awaken to become a child of God unless
you share the joy of knowing Christ with
them. Become the aroma of Christ.

CR

# What Should We Do?

*'I tell you the truth, whatever you did for one of the
least of these brothers of mine, you did for me.'*
Matthew 25:40

You see them on the streets of every
major city: the homeless. They live in a cul-
ture of their own in today's Western world
where they exist day-to-day in a world of
handouts and hand-me-downs. Their presence is a source of heated debates in many
cities, and no one seems to want them in
'my neighbourhood'.

Where do they come from, and what
should be done about them?

One answer can be found in the life of
P. W. Alexander and her essay *Christmas at
Home* where she reflects on her dedication
to community service – much of which
involves caring for the homeless. She
writes, 'As a child I did not look forward to
the holidays. It began with Halloween. In
the morning we went to church and in the

evening we collected for UNICEF. Thanksgiving and Christmas were equally painful. My mother would sign us all up to work at the soup kitchen.'[28]

Thus, she was raised in the art of serving, and as she grew older she began to understand better the reasons why her mother insisted that they care for others during the holidays. In fact, the closing words of her essay demonstrate the impact of her mother's actions.

*I do this not out of a sense of duty or obligation; I do it because it is my family tradition.*[29]

What special family traditions are you creating for your children?

છ

## Guess What?

*Let them ever shout for joy.*
*Psalm 5:11 KJV*

'Dad, Dad, guess what, guess what,' she screamed as she bounded into the room and jumped into her father's lap.

'What? What?' he responded with equal vigour and enthusiasm.

One of the greatest joys of his life was seeing his seven-year-old daughter Crystal's contagious love of life. In fact, she seemed to attack life with a voracious appetite for discovery unknown to him in any other child.

Before she could respond, he remembered a similar time two years earlier when Crystal came home from school with a brochure that described the coral reefs found in the Florida Keys. At that time she could not yet read, but her teacher had read the brochure to the class and she remembered it nearly word-for-word. A couple of weeks later, on a glass-bottom boat ride over the reefs, Crystal delighted everyone on board by identifying the types of coral even before the guide could point them out to the group. She wanted to share her newfound knowledge with everyone.

Shaking him from his reverie, Crystal announced with glee, 'My picture won first place in the County Art Fair!' His heart was overwhelmed with joy as he shared in her accomplishment. He was so proud of her. But, more importantly, he was so glad that God had blessed his life through Crystal, and he was delighted to hear her news.

God the Father also takes great joy in our accomplishments. Wouldn't it be great to rush into His presence, jump in His lap, and scream, 'Guess what, guess what,' whenever we achieve a life goal? Yes, He already knows, but still, He enjoys our thankfulness and loves our enthusiasm.

# Faith Is a Verb

*Now faith is the assurance of things hoped for,*
*the conviction of things not seen.*
*Hebrews 11:1 NASB*

*In You Can't Afford the Luxury of a*
*Negative Thought*, John Roger and Peter
McWilliams offered a new description of
faith. They chose the word *faithing* to
describe their proactive approach to confidence in life's outcomes.

In their thinking, faithing works in the
present, acknowledging that there is a purpose to everything and that life is unfolding
exactly as it should. It is actively trusting
that God can handle our troubles and needs
better than we can. All we must do is let
them go so that He can do His work.

### The Two Boxes

*I have in my hands two boxes*
*Which God gave me to hold.*

He said, 'Put all your sorrows in the black,
　And all your joys in the gold.'

I heeded His words, and in the two boxes
　Both my joys and sorrows I store,
But though the gold became heavier each day
　The black was as light as before.

With curiosity, I opened the black.
　I wanted to find out why
And I saw, in the base of the box, a hole
　Which my sorrows had fallen out by.

I showed the hole to God, and mused aloud,
　'I wonder where all my sorrows could be.'
He smiled a gentle smile at me.
　'My child, they're all here, with Me.'

I asked, 'God, why give me the boxes,
Why the gold, and the black with the hole?'
'My child, the gold is to count your blessings,
　the black is for you to let go.' [30]

❧

## *Moment of Truth*

> *Teach me thy way, O LORD; I will walk*
> *in thy truth.*
> Psalm 86:11 KJV

*W*ith these words, Jean Shepherd introduces a delightful and poignant essay dealing with the trials of adolescence, specifically blind dates:

*There are about four times in a man's life, or a woman's, too, for that matter, when unexpectedly, from out of the darkness, the blazing carbon lamp, the cosmic searchlight of Truth shines full upon them. It is how we react to those moments that forever seals our fate.*[31]

In the story, he is fourteen years old and agrees, against his better judgment, to go on a blind date.

The gist of the tale is that, contrary to all the logic of blind dates, his date, Junie Jo Prewitt, is beautiful. In fact, she 'made

Cleopatra look like a Girl Scout'. As the evening progresses however, he becomes aware that Junie Jo is *not* enjoying the date and in a moment of truth he realizes, 'I am the blind date.'[32] This is an extremely painful moment of truth where he faces that fact that where he was worried that his *date* might not be someone he would want to be with, the truth is that *he* is someone Junie Jo does not want to be seen with.

Shepherd concludes the story with the line: 'I didn't say much the rest of the night. There wasn't much to be said.'[33]

Life usually presents us with moments of truth – times when we have no choice but to see ourselves just as we really are. And, as Shepherd says, 'It is how we react in those moments that really matters.'

Moments of truth come each day. When these moments do come, we need to seek guidance and act with humility. For we are only as spiritual as our last decision.

ೞ

# Seeing with the Heart

*So give your servant a discerning heart.*
*1 Kings 3:9*

*M*aria was a kindhearted teacher's helper who simply wanted to 'love the children better' in this class for emotionally disturbed students. She could tolerate much, but Danny was wearing her patience out. It had been easier to love him before, when he would try to hurt himself rather than others. And, although Danny was only seven years old, it really hurt when he hit her.

For many months Danny had been withdrawing into a private world and trying to hit his head against a wall whenever he got upset. But now, he was making 'progress', because instead of withdrawing, he was striking out at Maria.

'Progress?' exclaimed Maria. 'How is it progress for him to want to hurt me?'

'Danny was repeatedly abused as a small

child,' explained the school psychologist. 'He has known only adults who were mean to him or simply ignored his most basic needs. He has had no one he could trust. No one to hold him close; no one to dry his tears when he cried or fix him food when he was hungry. He has been punished for no reason. He's making progress, because for the first time in his life, he trusts an adult enough to act out his anger rather than self-destruct. You are that trustworthy adult, Maria.'

Upon hearing this explanation, Maria, with tears spilling from her eyes, exclaimed, 'I see!' As comprehension dawned, her anger quickly melted.

John Ruskin wrote, 'When love and skill work together, expect a masterpiece.'[34] Sometimes progress seems elusive, but God is faithful to continue the good work He has started in each of our lives. If we will open the eyes of our hearts, we will see His hand at work in our midst.

## Grace Tickets

*'And the one who comes to Me I will certainly
not cast out.'*
John 6:37 NASB

*A* Bible teacher talked about God's
'Grace Tickets'. She said God makes
Himself available to us no matter how
many times we reach out for an extra
Grace Ticket. His grace is available to us in
liberal amounts. She even prayed that she
would have the wisdom to know when to
reach out and take another.

When the alarm goes off at 5:30 am, it is
all too easy to slip a hand from under the
covers and push that snooze button to
allow for ten more minutes of sleep. You
might repeat the same involuntary movement every ten minutes until 6 am when the
clock radio is programmed to come on.

The minute the announcer's voice is
heard, you are immediately jolted from bed
realizing you have overslept and must do in

twenty minutes what would normally take fifty. The antics that take place in that room are worthy of a feature on a television comedy show.

We all need several of God's Grace Tickets for times in our lives when we attempt to put God and His timing on hold. Yet God has made Himself available to us every minute of the day. We are privileged to call out to Him no matter how severe or minuscule our situation. His grace is sufficient for each of us – at all times. He never runs out. It is up to us to open our eyes each morning and reach out to the Giver of all Grace Tickets.

Many of us are in the habit of pushing the 'snooze button' on God's time. However, He is patiently waiting with a whole stack of Grace Tickets for us. Why not set your clock by His?

# The Birthday Surprise

*Let all that you do be done with love.*
*1 Corinthians 16:14 NKJV*

It was one of those dreadful evenings
every family experiences on occasion.
Though it was Saturday night – and a pre-
birthday celebration at that – nothing was
going right. Even the ride home from dinner out was lousy.

Dad was angry from watching too many
political shows on television. The seventeen-
year-old thought his life was over because
he hadn't had driving lessons yet, and
couldn't get his licence. The eleven-year-old
was yelling because the seventeen-year-old
punched him for . . . well, nobody quite
knew why.

And Mum was angry that she had just
spent good money on a nice restaurant meal
for these ungrateful monsters.

On arriving home, she grudgingly decided to start the birthday preparations and

went to the kitchen to lay out ingredients for her elder son's favourite cake. Within ten minutes, almost magically, the mood of the entire family changed.

The seventeen-year-old walked into the kitchen, saw the task at hand, and hugged his mum for making his cake, even after his poor behaviour. The eleven-year-old was excited because Mum let him help mix the cake. Dad was happy because everyone else had stopped fighting.

And Mum was amazed that the whole evening turned on the baking of a cake – a small act of love.

We can never guess how important our slightest actions will be to those around us. As you go through the day, you have a choice in your interactions with everyone you meet. Choose the act of love.

ॐ

## Perfect Harmony

*A man who has friends must himself be friendly,
but there is a friend who sticks closer than a brother.*
Proverbs 18:24 NKJV

The late Leonard Bernstein — conductor, composer, teacher and advocate — may well be the most important figure in American music of the twentieth century. With his personality and passion for his favourite subject, he inspired generations of new musicians and taught thousands that music should be an integral part of everyone's life.

As a public figure, Bernstein was larger-than-life – his charm and persuasiveness infectious. While his career progressed, he was constantly sought after for performances, lectures and other appearances.

But it's said that in his later years, one way his personal life eroded was in his friendships. There came a time when he had few close friends. After his death, a comment from one of his longest acquaintances was that 'you wanted to be his friend, but so many other people sought his attention that, eventually, the friendliest thing you could do was leave him alone.'[35]

Scientific evidence now shows us how important friendships are, not only to our emotional health, but physical and mental health as well. But these most cherished relationships are a two-way street. A few tips for keeping friendships on track are:

Be aware of your friends' likes and dis-likes. Remember your friends' birthdays and anniversaries. Take interest in your friends' children. Become need sensitive. Keep in touch by phone. Express what you like about your relationship with another person. Serve your friends in thoughtful, unexpected ways.[36]

Good friends are gifts from God. Is there someone you need to call today?

# Shining Light

*Let your light shine before men in such a way that they may see your good works, and glorify your Father who is in heaven.*
*Matthew 5:16 NASB*

Upon waking in the morning, most of us have regular duties we follow or some established routine to make ourselves presentable for the day. Many of us would never allow certain friends or relatives to see us when we first crawl out of bed. Most of us would rather die than to have the 'real us' exposed before we have showered, shaved, made up our faces and hair and brushed our teeth.

Although there is nothing wrong with wanting to present ourselves looking our best, there needs to also be something on the inside that radiates Christ in us.

When a piece of coal is placed on top of a sizzling hot bed of ashes it soon catches the flame and begins to burn in brilliant colours as it radiates heat for long periods of time. However, if we took that same piece of coal away from the flame, it would quickly lose its glow and burn out. The brilliance would disappear and the heat from it would rapidly diminish. Nothing would be left except a big, black, useless lump.

We become useless without a fresh daily infusion of His power and grace. Beginning the day in the presence of the Lord guarantees that His light will shine through us before men with a brilliance. Sitting at His feet and allowing Him to be our teacher before the day begins provides us with the spark that exposes areas of our lives in which the Lord needs to do His cleansing or healing work.

## What of Walls?

*The wall of Jerusalem also is broken down.*
*Nehemiah 1:3 KJV*

*T*he following lines from poet Robert Frost's famous work 'Mending Wall' hit right at the heart of the challenge of maintaining proper relationships:

*I let my neighbor know beyond the hill;*
*And on a day we meet to walk the line*
*And set the wall between us once again.*[37]

The poem both celebrates tradition and pokes fun at it at the same time. Many individuals, over the years, have debated its most famous line: 'Good fences make good neighbours.'

Frost himself takes issue with the need for carefully maintained boundaries when he attempts to get a rise out of his neighbour by asking, 'Why do they make good neighbours?'

Getting no response, he goes on to say, 'Something there is that doesn't love a wall, that wants it down.' Still no response, and in the closing lines he likens his neighbour to 'an old stone savage armed, who will not go behind his father's saying'.

Why do we seem to always be building walls between others and ourselves or between God and ourselves? Is it perhaps because we fear becoming vulnerable to rejection? Or do we simply feel an irresistible need to stake our claim to what we want as our own? In either case, it takes much courage to maintain proper respect for one another without building walls that separate us inappropriately.

Robert Frost urges us to be careful to know what we might be 'walling in or out and to whom we might give offense' upon building walls. Walls are serious business and we need to be careful how we use them. Done wrong, they create inequality and hatred. Done right, they can make for good relationships.

&#8706;

## Determined Choice

*So give your servant a discerning heart.*
*1 Kings 3:9*

'Please understand that there are times when the body, for some reason or another, will spontaneously abort the foetus.'

The world seemed to stop dead still for Jim and Donna as they listened to her doctor. Donna, in just her fourth month, had begun to haemorrhage earlier in the day. When they came to Dr Joseph's surgery they were concerned; now, they were becoming very frightened.

'It is nothing that you have done or not done,' continued Dr Joseph, 'but, we want to send you down for an immediate ultrasound to see how things are doing. I want you to know that if your body has decided to abort the foetus it is for a good reason. But, let's wait until we know for sure.'

With those parting words, Jim and Donna headed to the lab for the ultrasound test.

'Jim, Jim, can you see the baby? He's right there! He's OK, he's OK!' shouted Donna as soon as the technician showed them the form of their baby on the monitor, and they could clearly see its heart beating. The baby was indeed still alive; Donna's body had not aborted him. They were overwhelmed with relief.

Five months later their first son was born, and another miracle took place as he survived complications during the birth. Upon finally bringing their 'miracle boy' home, they both agreed that God must have something really special in store for him.

Where had such faith come from? Determined choice, perhaps. As Oswald Chambers once said, 'Faith is deliberate confidence in the character of God whose ways you may not understand at the time.'[38]

## *As God Is My Witness . . .*

> *But He gives a greater grace. Therefore it says,*
> *'God is opposed to the proud, but gives*
> *grace to the humble.'*
> *James 4:6 NASB*

To some, there was one devastatingly funny episode of the 1980s television comedy series *WKRP in Cincinnati.* Set in a small Ohio radio station at Thanksgiving, the plot involved a promotion in which the advertising manager decided to give away free turkeys to customers patronizing a local shopping centre.

As they planned a giveaway circus, complete with aeroplane fly-overs and a live remote news setup, the staff was certain this would be their most successful promotional campaign ever.

But the station manager soon learned that, once again, he had overestimated the basic intelligence of his ad manager. *WKRP* fans will long remember the chaotic radio

broadcast as terrified customers and shop-
keepers ran screaming, dodging the live
turkeys which were, in the words of the
quivering news reporter, 'dropping like
bags of wet cement', as they were tossed
from the aeroplane circling above the shopping centre.

And few viewers will forget the stunned
look on the station manager's face as his
abashed and bewildered ad man held his
hand up to swear, 'As God is my witness, *I
thought turkeys could fly!*'

With a little luck, the most important lesson we learn is that we may not know
everything, so it's good to ask questions.
And that's where God's wonderful gift of
humility comes in. Don't be ashamed to
find out what you don't know – just
remember the turkeys.

CR

## *Hidden Blessings*

*In everything give thanks; for this is the
will of God in Christ Jesus for you.
1 Thessalonians 5:18 NKJV*

It was a rough day at the office. Nancy
was struggling with too many meetings, too
many project deadlines, and not enough
time to complete anything. Her performance review was due and she feared the rise
she needed was not going to happen.

What's more, her daughter had been off
school with flu for three days with no sign
of improvement. Nancy and her husband
Tom were rotating their office leave so
someone would always be home with their
child.

Her phone rang. It was Tom calling,
worried because their daughter's breathing
was becoming laboured. Nancy knew
immediately that the child needed to see a
doctor again, and she had to be there with
her.

Racing home, she wanted to cry. Why did everything have to happen at once? And when would she ever get a break?

Suddenly, she was startled by a loud bang, as the car ahead of her blew a tyre and slowly manoeuvred to a nearby parking area. Nancy took a deep breath to regain her composure and thought, 'OK, God, how bad off am I, really?'

As she picked up her daughter and sped to the emergency clinic, Nancy decided to concentrate on the things that were going right.

*Thank You for good tyres and cars that work.*
*Thank You for my job.*
*Thank You for doctors.*
*Thank You for insurance.*
*Thank You for helping her to breathe.*
*Thank You for coming with me.*
*Thank You for showing me how much I have to be thankful for.*

❧

## Rules. What Rules?

*Blessed are the peacemakers: for they
shall be called the children of God.*
Matthew 5:9 KJV

'What do you mean, you don't have to
go by rules?' Rick asked his daughter
Heather, with a note of incredulity in his
voice.

'Shelley said that we don't have to go by
rules,' she responded.

'Well, Shelley's wrong, you do have to go
by rules.'

'No, I don't, Shelley said so.'

'Yes, you do!'

The argument continued for a few minutes until Rick's wife Jane stepped into
Heather's bedroom and quietly said, 'Rick,
do you realize that you are arguing with a
three-year-old?' She then turned to their
little girl and asked, 'Heather, do you know
what rules are?'

'No.'

'When you are at school do you and Shelley ever need to line up so that your class can go to lunch or out to the playground?'

'Yes.'

'That's a rule.'

'OK.'

With a small smile, Jane hugged Heather and quietly left the room. A sheepish look on his face, Rick followed. 'I guess I got carried away,' he mumbled.

It's pretty easy to get carried away. In fact, if we are not careful we can find ourselves embroiled in conflict with others without ever knowing why. Family feuds are often like that; the reason for the hatred has long since been forgotten, but the animosity continues from generation to generation. Continuing in such conflict without trying to understand one another is as senseless as Rick arguing with his three-year-old.

It took the loving voice of Heather's mother, Rick's wife, to calm the waters. We can be that voice too if we so desire. Remember, Jesus said, 'Blessed are the peacemakers.'

ᕼ

# Dr Simpson and Dancing

*And he has inspired him to teach.*
*Exodus 35:34 NRSV*

Lively music filled the air as the college students mingled with one another, shared laughs and danced together. Just then, Dr Simpson walked up to Rob and asked him, 'Why aren't you out there dancing with everyone else?'

'I don't want anyone to laugh at me,' he responded.

'What makes you think that they would be looking at you anyway?' came her quick retort with more than a hint of laughter in her voice. She was like that. Quick to challenge her students' assumptions, but in a way that provoked thought and self-examination rather than pain and embarrassment.

A respected and admired professor of English, Dr Simpson expected much from every student. She was tough, but her classes were always full. It was exchanges

like this one that made it possible for Rob
to see his life from a perspective other than
his own, and in gaining this insight he
became more self-confident and less
uptight. She helped – no, she forced him to
grow as both a student and a person. Dr
Simpson epitomized the role of teacher.

In the words of one author, 'The teacher
must be able to discern when to push and
when to comfort, when to chastise and
when to praise, when to challenge and
when to hold back, when to encourage risk
and when to protect.'[39] This, Dr Simpson
did on a daily basis. And this is just the
type of teacher we need. God usually provides each of us with our own unique Dr
Simpson – many times with more than one.

Can you recall your favourite teacher(s)?
And, did she or he challenge you to become
more than you were before? Thank God,
they did!

$\text{CR}$

## Proper Form

*But as He who called you is holy, you also*
*be holy in all your conduct, because it*
*is written, 'Be holy, for I am holy.'*
1 Peter 1:15,16 NKJV

A father tells the story of an afternoon once spent with his three-year-old daughter. An avid golfer, he was practising with his clubs in the garden while she played nearby. As he prepared for each swing, he would look to his left to aim the shot, then back to his right to make sure the child was out of harm's way – only then would he take his shot.

Soon, he noticed that his daughter was also 'playing golf'. She had taken a stick to use as a club, and he watched as she set her 'club', carefully looked left, then right, then took her shot. In her perception, proper golfing form required that you look both ways before you swing.

Whether we realize it or not, our example leaves an impression on others. In the 1800s, English minister Charles Spurgeon put it this way:

*A man's life is always more forcible than his speech. When men take stock of him they reckon his deeds as pounds and his words as pennies. If his life and doctrine disagree the mass of onlookers accept his practice and reject his preaching.*

When Jesus said, 'You are the light of the world,' He wasn't speaking only of our verbal witness. The most profound message we will ever send is the one we live on a day-to-day basis. And it's never more important than when we don't know anyone is paying attention.

Because Someone is always paying attention.

CR

## *The Effective Optimist*

*Rejoicing in hope, patient in tribulation,*
*continuing steadfastly in prayer.*
*Romans 12:12 NKJV*

A Hasidic story tells of Rabbi Naftali of Ropchitz, known for his persistence – and for his wit. One day, he remained in the synagogue an entire morning, praying that the rich would give more of their money to the poor.

When he returned home, his wife asked him, 'Were you successful with your prayer?'

Rabbi Naftali answered with a smile, 'I am halfway there!' His wife looked puzzled.

'Oh, yes,' he assured her. 'The poor have agreed to accept!'[40]

Optimism is one of the greatest gifts of human nature. Many of civilization's achievements can be traced – not to the highest intellects or talents – but to perseverance and positive thinking.

It's a misconception that optimism requires no more than a sunny assumption that things will be fine. Real optimists rarely sit back and wait. Attitude is only the beginning.

George Bernard Shaw once said, 'People are always blaming their circumstances for what they are. I don't believe in circumstances. The people who get on in this world are the people who get up and look for the circumstances they want, and if they can't find them . . . they make them!'

Positive thinkers can't guarantee that things will go well, but they use every available resource to help make their goal a reality, including – and especially – prayer.

There is no more hopeful time than morning, when the day is new and full of promise. What are your challenges today? Ask for God's help in pointing out the hidden opportunities. It's the first step to becoming an effective optimist.

☙

# A Photographic Memory

*If we confess our sins, He is faithful and just
to forgive us our sins and to cleanse us
from all unrighteousness.*
1 John 1:9 NKJV

Famed photographer and conservationist Ansel Adams was known for his visionary photos of western landscapes, inspired by a boyhood trip to Yosemite National Park. His love of nature's raw perfection was apparent in his stark, mysterious black-and-white wilderness photos.

In 1944, he shot a beautiful scene, later entitled 'Winter Sunrise: The Sierra Nevada, from Lone Pine, California'. It portrayed the craggy Sierra mountains in the bright morning sunlight, a small dark horse appearing in the foothills.

But the story is told that, later, as Adams developed the negative, he noticed an 'LP' carved in the hillside. Apparently, some local high school teenagers had etched their initials on the mountain.

Intent on recapturing nature's original, he took a brush and ink and carefully removed the initials from his negative. The man who gave the Sierra Club its look believed in preserving, even perfecting nature, in life as well as in photography.[41]

Ansel Adams probably never gave a second thought to the unsightly scar on the mountain in his photo creation. In his mind's eye, he saw the beauty of the original and took steps to bring that beauty back into focus.

Someone once observed that 'the purpose of the cross is to repair the irreparable'. Through the blood of Christ, we know that our sins have been forgiven – our scars erased – and that once removed, our sins are forgotten. The Lord remembers them no more. When we are willing to confess our sins, He takes joy in restoring us to our original beauty.

03

# Gentle Ripples

*O, God, You are my God; Early will I seek You.*
*Psalm 63:1 NKJV*

Early in the morning a lake is usually
very still; no animals, no people, no noise,
no boats, no cars. All is quiet.

This is the best time to skim stones. By
taking a small flat pebble and throwing it at
the right angle, you can skim it across the
water leaving circles of ripples every time it
makes contact with the lake. The ripples
form small and very defined circles at first,
then they spread out and break apart until
they vanish. If several people skim stones at
the same time, the ripples cross over one
another and blend together to make mini-
waves across the lake. The impact can be
pretty amazing.

For most of us, mornings are filled with
so many things that need our attention that
we find it difficult to spend time alone with
God. However, the Lord set a marvellous

example for us by rising early to listen to God. If we make no time for this quiet morning time with God, we often find there is also no time during the day. Then we end up going to bed with regret or guilt. Maybe tomorrow, we think. But many times, tomorrow never comes.

When we spend time alone with God at the beginning of each day, we become acquainted with Him and start becoming like Him. Throughout our days, the ripple effect of our time with God in the early morning will impact the lives of those with whom we have contact.

When these ripples blend with others who spend time with God, we create mini-waves of love and joy. It all starts with a quiet time and a gentle ripple.

ભ

## Pushing the Rock

*He will comfort us in the labour and painful
toil of our hands.*
*Genesis 5:29*

*I*n one of the Greek myths, an ancient
character named Sisyphus constantly pushes
a large rock up a hill never quite reaching
the top. As he nears his goal, he always
loses strength and lets go of the rock only
to watch it roll back to the foot of the hill.
He then returns to the bottom of the hill
and begins pushing it towards the top
again.

Unfortunately, this may be how many of
us see our journey towards spiritual maturi-
ty. Each failure, each new sin, means that
we must begin anew in our relationship
with Him. Thus, a 'victorious walk' for
Christ becomes instead a never-ending itin-
erary of 'starting over'. In fact, if we are not
careful, we will think that we have to push
the rock (our spirituality and successful

Christian living) to the top of the hill all by ourselves (thus gaining the presence of God and a successful Christian life).

This is not true because all we really need to do is allow Christ to put His hands over ours to use His strength to push the rock. When we do this, the rock will never roll to the bottom of the hill, not even when we fall short of the high ideals of the Christian life.

You see, failure does not arbitrarily demand that we return to the bottom of the hill; instead, God is always with us wherever we are and He will lead us onwards in our walk with Him. If you are tempted to get discouraged when things don't seem to work right, remember Sisyphus and the words of Frederick W. Robertson: 'In God's world, for those who are in earnest, there is no failure.'[42]

## *Everyday Grace*

*Every good gift and every perfect gift is from above,*
*and comes down from the Father of lights, with*
*whom there is no variation or shadow of turning.*
*James 1:17 NKJV*

*I*n his book, *Come As You Are*, G. Peter
Fleck relates a satire of the Sermon on the
Mount that could easily occur today:

> *Then Jesus took His disciples up the moun-*
> *tain and gathering them around Him, He*
> *taught them, saying:*
> > *'Blessed are the poor in spirit,*
> > *for theirs is the kingdom of heaven.*
> > *Blessed are the meek.*
> > *Blessed are they that mourn.*
> > *Blessed are the merciful.*
> > *Blessed are they who thirst for justice.*
> > *Blessed are you who are persecuted.*
> > *Blessed are you when you suffer.*
> *Be glad and rejoice for great is your reward in*
> *Heaven and remember what I am telling you.'*

*Then Simon Peter said,*
  *'Do we have to write this down?'...*
*And James said,*
  *'Will we have a test on this?'...*
*And Bartholomew said,*
  *'Do we have to turn this in?'...*
*And John said,*
  *'The other disciples didn't have to learn
this.'...*
*And Judas said,*
  *'What does this have to do with real life?'*[43]

In the author's words, 'Grace had gone
unrecognized.'

Indeed, we experience God's grace regularly – but do we recognize it? Fleck
defines grace as '. . . a blessing that is unexpected . . . that brings a sense of the divine
order of things into our lives.'

Do you notice the *everyday grace* in life? It
comes at the oddest moments, in the words
of children, a good idea when needed, a call
from a friend when it's least expected.

As you prepare for a new day, open your
eyes to everyday grace. It is God's way of
saying, 'I am here.'

## Walk the Walk

*The just man walketh in his integrity.*
*Proverbs 20:7 KJV*

Sir Winston Churchill, the irascible leader of Britain during World War II, is one of the most well-known world leaders of modern times. What many people forget is that he is also associated with one of the most ignoble defeats in modern British history – the disastrous Gallipoli campaign of World War I that forced his resignation from the Admiralty in 1915 and nearly destroyed his career.[44]

Did he give up? Not Sir Winston Churchill! In fact, twenty-five years later on May 10, 1940, he succeeded Chamberlain as Prime Minister. The days that followed however are considered among the darkest of all British history.

World War II brought with it Dunkirk and the fall of France. London found itself bombed nightly by the famous blitz. It was precisely during these times that Churchill 'urged his compatriots to conduct themselves so that, "if the British Empire and its Commonwealth last for a thousand years, men will still say, 'This was their finest hour.' " '[45]

Did Churchill ever have doubts about the outcome of the world conflict that threatened to destroy all that he loved? It would be only human. Regardless, he lived his challenge to his countrymen. He did indeed conduct himself so historians consider that time to be 'his finest hour'. In simple terms, 'He walked the walk and talked the talk.'

In that sense, Churchill and other world leaders we admire are really not so different from each of us. We, too, are challenged to live every day with integrity and consistency. And we are just as capable of living our lives so that it can be said of us that when we were faced with challenges, it was our finest hour.

# We Are Equal, You and I

*Be at rest once more, O my soul.*
Psalm 116:7

*I*magine that you are a 21-year-old young man, father of a baby son, and on your way to divorce. You have been raised in a church your entire life where divorce is 'a failure to be prayed for but avoided'. Now, *you* are a divorcé. You are that failure who is unclean. With that mind-set, Horace scheduled an appointment to speak with his pastor.

Pastor Hale met Horace at the door of his office with a warm smile and firm handshake. Much to Horace's surprise, he did not direct him to the chair in front of his desk and return to his high-backed leather seat behind it. Instead, the pastor took his seat in a comfortable chair and motioned for Horace to sit on the adjacent couch. This simple gesture of sitting without a desk between them overwhelmed Horace.

To Horace's way of thinking, the pastor was holy and he was unfit. Yet, here he was being treated as though his needs were the only thing the pastor was interested in. His actions said, 'I do not consider myself better than you simply because God has called me to serve as pastor for this church. I am here to serve you, and I want you to feel comfortable because you are important to me just as you are today.'

Horace's torment and doubt began to ease. A sense of rest and assurance comforted his hurting heart.

Although divorce is commonplace in today's world, this does nothing to minimise its pain for those experiencing it. If you have the chance, be a Pastor Hale to a Horace today — your life and theirs will be all the richer for your caring.

❧

# *Enjoyment without Winning?*
# *You Bet!*

*Shout for joy to the LORD.*
*Psalm 100:1*

*T*he two boys were acquaintances but not friends. In fact, you could easily consider them rivals. Steve was the stereotypical young athlete who was stronger, taller, faster and better than most of his peers. Don was smaller and slower but filled with dogged determination and an intense desire to win. One evening during a Little League baseball game, a most remarkable event happened for the two young boys.

Steve had pitched a 'no-hitter' the previous week and his team was leading by one run at the bottom of the last innings when Don came up to bat. With runners on first and second base and two outs, Don needed to get a base hit for his team to win. The encounter was a challenging one with Steve nearly hitting Don with the first pitch.

From that moment on, adrenaline surging, Don proceeded to swing mightily at the next three pitches – missing each one and striking out.

But to the surprise of everyone watching, the final strike and the end of the game found Don striding towards the mound, a goofy grin on his face and his bat forgotten in his left hand, with his right hand outstretched to shake hands with Steve. Steve came striding off the mound to meet him with his own hand outstretched and a small smile on his lips – not a smug grin of triumph but a warm, delightful smile of a secret shared.

What happened? For just a moment, the joy of participating in the game superseded the need to win the game. Life can be like that, too. With the right approach, the joy of living can countermand the need to win because we begin to trust God with the outcome while we enjoy the process.

❈

# *Sheila*

*Be not forgetful to entertain strangers.*
*Hebrews 13:2 KJV*

*S*heila paused at the door of the small country church, uncertain. *It's so quiet in here,* she thought. *I will just sit and rest for a moment, and then I will be on my way.* She didn't mean to fall asleep, it was just so warm and comfortable and she was so tired.

As she settled into the back pew, the air included the slight mustiness of worn rugs mixed with the smell of furniture polish, and dust mites danced in the sunbeams coming through the broad windows. As her eyelids grew heavy, she could hear the building settle with minute creaks and groans. Somewhere in the sunshine outside, she heard the sparkling laughter of a young child at play. Then her eyes closed and she slept.

The young pastor came from his study

near the front of the church and was heading to the parsonage. He was surprised to see her there on the back pew, head resting against the high end piece, sound asleep.

*Why, she can't be more than fourteen or fifteen. She must have run away from home,* he thought.

Slipping out quietly, he went next door to the parsonage and asked his wife Brenda to come back to the church with him. Brenda gently awakened Sheila. Although she was embarrassed to be found sleeping in the church, Sheila quickly responded to the gentle love and concern of Brenda. Food, shelter, clothing and prayerful compassion were offered to Sheila. In the years to come, she often thought of that small church and the caring couple she met there.

It was a memory she savoured. As she moved from shelter to shelter, she would often tell anyone who would listen that on one occasion she met Jesus and His name was Brenda.

∞

# Rocking Chairs

*I lift up my eyes to the hills.*
Psalm 121:1

The centre is getting a little long in the tooth, but the view remains unchanged – majestic and peaceful. It is located outside Knoxville, Tennessee in the foothills of the Great Smoky Mountains. A small conference centre is built on the crest of a hill overlooking a mountain valley. The building has two storeys, and the top one includes a meeting room of some renown.

This meeting room is fairly large with low ceilings and large windows on the eastern wall. Inside it, you find a number of rocking chairs in a large circle with braided rugs on the hardwood floors. Over the years, different groups have met in that room to examine community issues – controversial ones usually – ones where you could easily expect anger and disagreement. But the impact of the rocking chairs has always been the same; they create an environment that promotes easy conversation mixed with quiet meditation.

Somehow, it is difficult to work up a heated argument when you are rocking in a rocking chair and gazing out of the window across that long valley to see the majesty of Grandfather Mountain rising in the distance. Tranquillity becomes the norm during those times.

It is really hard to argue when you share solitude and rocking chairs with other people. Isaac Taylor said: 'A man of meditation is happy, not for an hour or a day, but quite round the circle of all his years.'

Perhaps we should consider investing more in rocking chairs and quiet times. One might even wonder if Isaac spent some time in a rocking chair.

CR

# The Work of the Potter

*Then I went down to the potter's house, and, behold,
he wrought a work on the wheels.*
*Jeremiah 18:3 KJV*

Have you ever watched a potter begin to
shape a vessel? It is a most amazing sight,
because the potter will only succeed if he
gets the unformed chunk of clay in the
exact centre of the wheel. Once the clay is
centred, the skill of the potter can be
realised.

The potter carefully wets his hands,
selects his clay and places it on the wheel.
As he begins to turn the wheel, the lumps
in the clay are revealed. Spinning the wheel
faster, he smoothes out the lumps, and the
clay begins to take on an unruffled appearance.

This is just the first part of the task. We
now see him shape the mass of clay so that
its heart is perfectly aligned with the very
centre of the wheel. This requires both

strength and a loving, delicate touch. This 'centring' is the most important step in the preparation process, because it gives the piece strength and integrity.

Our spiritual walk with God is just like this. We begin as a hunk of clay with many lumps, and through God's grace and skill, we are transformed into beautiful, strong vessels for the kingdom. But we must align our very heart with the centre of God's will. God is always at work in our lives, especially during the times of proper preparation.

Henry Ward Beecher said, 'We are always on the anvil; by trials God is shaping us for higher things.'[46] Of this you can rest assured: When you allow God to shape you, He will always use you for good.

∽

# Thank You, Lord

*I will give thanks to the LORD with all my heart.*
Psalm 9:1 NASB

It is easier to thank the Lord after we have seen His work. We have something to go back to and rejoice over. It is not as easy to be thankful for what we don't see or haven't experienced.

A mother purchased a new violin for her son. Together they had saved for months to be able to afford this fine instrument. He had promised to care for it, but it wasn't long before the boy had forgotten his promise and left his violin out on the porch overnight. The cold night air and the heavy morning dew caused the violin to bulge and the sound quality was no longer the same.

The boy's mother took this opportunity to teach her son a lesson for life. She decided to show her son what went into the making of the violin. She took him to the store where they had made the purchase, they visited a manufacturing company where violins were produced and went to a lumber mill where the wood had been carefully chosen for such a fine instrument. They even visited a forest where trees were being grown specifically for quality instruments. The mother and son also made trips to learn how the bow and strings were manufactured. She wanted her son to understand why he should be thankful for the beautiful musical instrument with which he had been blessed.

God wants our thanks, and He has provided us with a never-ending supply of reminders of why we should be grateful to Him. Starting the day off in an attitude of gratefulness leaves little room for complaints and much room for grace to flourish.

CR

# *Stay with Your Father*

> *I am with you and will watch over you*
> *wherever you go.*
> *Genesis 28:15*

Eleven-year-old Bobby was having the time of his life on the hiking trip. He, his father, two brothers and uncle were all on a day hike to Blue Lake, four miles high into a wilderness area. The trail, as most mountain trails do, led upwards by winding around and through tall pine trees. Occasionally, the trail would break out into small clearings and cross crystal-clear streams.

Bobby was determined to be the first person to the lake. The path was plainly marked and easy to follow, so he quickly pushed ahead of the small group. The sounds of the group's easy banter soon faded and suddenly he found himself surrounded by stillness. He was alone. He was so far ahead of the group that he was out of sight and hearing distance.

The beautiful morning began to take on an ominous air. What if a bear were in the woods? What if some mountain man, gone crazy, was waiting with a hatchet in the trees? What if . . .

In a moment Bobby decided he would rather be with the group; he turned around and headed back down the path to meet them. In just a couple of minutes he was with them again. Safe!

Sometimes we get so anxious to be first that we run off ahead of everyone important to us. We can even get so far from God by relying on our own knowledge or expertise that we place ourselves in dangerous circumstances. At that moment – and the moment will surely come when we realise how alone we are – we can always return to the safety of being with the Father.

ෙ

## Inner Light

*Not that I speak in respect of want: for I have
learned, in whatsoever state I am,
therewith to be content.*
Philippians 4:11,12 KJV

*I*n Barrow, Alaska, morning takes on a
whole new meaning. At 330 miles from the
Arctic Circle and almost as close to the
North Pole, Barrow is the real-life 'Land of
the Midnight Sun'. For eighty-three days,
from May 11 to August 1, the sun never
sinks below the horizon.

But there's also the dark side to life at
high latitudes. Each year on November 18,
residents watch the sun dip below the horizon, the last sunset of the year for more
than two months.

While not pitch-black all the time, winter
in Barrow is truly a season of darkness.
Temperatures dip so low that fuel oil con-
geals. Keys snap like toothpicks in frozen
locks. Windchills near 100 below can cause

frostbite in thirty seconds.

The perpetual dark, cold and wind can seem oppressive to those who take the daily blush of the sun for granted. Residents admit that dreaming of Hawaii is pretty common.

Not everyone wants to leave, though. 'Many people here truly like the winter, enjoying the peace and quiet,' says Barrow Mayor, Jim Vorderstrasse. 'A lot of it reflects on a person's outlook on life. You can sit around being depressed, or you can get up and find something worthwhile to do.'[47]

Seasons of darkness can occur in anyone's life. And how we get through those difficult times depends on our outlook. We can shut ourselves in and yearn for another life, or we can rely on God's Light to help us find a life of hope and serenity. The choice is always ours.

ᘓ

## God's Promises

*But seek first His kingdom and His righteousness;*
*and all these things shall be added to you.*
*Matthew 6:33 NASB*

*O*ur society is inundated with hundreds of reasons why being first is a goal to be obtained. It is necessary to be first in every line to get the best seat. Winning first place carries the most weight, the largest purse, and the most recognition. Rarely are we able to recall the second runner-up in any event. No doubt about it, first is the crème de la crème. Or is it?

There is nothing wrong with obtaining first place status. As a matter of fact, the Bible encourages us to set high goals and reach for them with perseverance. Each of us knows people we admire because of the goals they have set and reached through committed determination. But what about those who do their very best and never make the first string, never get the top

200

grade, never win the trophy, etc.? What do they do with God's promises?

God has a plan for each of us. The stakes are often very high. The game plan will be interrupted many times by the devil. We will doubt, be discouraged and face what seem to be impossibilities. However, God promises us that if we seek Him first, we have whatever we need – *all* of His blessings and *all* of His promises.

It takes faith! Some never make it to the finish line, yet their labour is rewarded because they did their best. The contributions of those on the sidelines or behind the scenes are rewarded, although not with a shiny plaque they can display.

Each of us can place first if we simply believe the promises of God and become dead to doubt, dumb to discouragement, and blind to impossibilities.

ᴄʀ

# References

Unless otherwise indicated, all Scripture quotations are taken from the *Holy Bible, New International Version*® NIV®. Copyright © 1973, 1978, 1984 by International Bible Society. Used by permission of Zondervan Publishing House. All rights reserved.

Scripture quotations marked NKJV are taken from *The New King James Version* of the Bible. Copyright © 1979, 1980, 1982, 1994 by Thomas Nelson, Inc., Publisher. Used by permission.

Scripture quotations marked KJV are taken from the *King James Version* of the Bible.

Scripture quotations marked NASB are taken from the *New American Standard Bible*. Copyright © 1960, 1962, 1963, 1968, 1971, 1972, 1973, 1975, 1977 by The Lockman Foundation. Used by permission.

Scripture quotations marked ASV are taken from the *American Standard Version*. Copyright © 1901 by Thomas Nelson and Sons and copyright © 1929 by International Council of Religious Education.

Scripture quotations marked NRSV are taken from the *New Revised Standard Version* of the Bible. Copyright © 1989 by The Division of Christian Education of the National Council of the Churches of Christ in the USA. Used by permission. All rights reserved.

## Endnotes

1. *The Diary of a Young Girl*, Anne Frank (New York: Doubleday, 1952).

2. Ibid.

3. Kovachevich Radomir.

4 Author unknown.

5. *Daily Bread*, July 20, 1992.

6. *Reader's Digest*, March 1999, p 117.

7. 'Self-Esteem', Mike Nichols, *The Complete Book of Everyday Christianity*, Robert Banks and R. Paul Stevens, eds. (Downers Grove, IL: Intervarsity Press, 1997) p 872.

8. *Who Said That?* George Sweeting (Chicago, IL: Moody Press, 1995).

9. Ibid.

10. Marilyn Elias, Volunteer pilots wing patients to hospitals, *USA Today*, June 10 1996, p 04D.

11. *Newsweek*, February 15, 1999, p 47.

12. Jim Gleason (Transplant Recipient Support List: trnsplnt@wuvmd.wustl.edu).

13. The Misheard Lyrics Website, www.kissthisguy.com.

14. *Today in the Word*, February 1991, p 10.

15. *Christianity Today*, December 9, 1996, Vol. 40, No. 14, p 80.

16 *Today in the Word*, September 2, 1992.

17 Maya Angelou, *Wouldn't Take Nothin' for My Journey Now* (New York: Random House,

1993) p 62.

18  Barbara Hatcher, *Vital Speeches*, March 1, 1987.

19  Judy Seymour, 'The Freeway Not Taken: Lake Route Worth the Slower Pace,' *Minneapolis Star Tribune*, May 12 1997, p 15A.

20  *Today in the Word*, Moody Bible Institute, January 1992, p 8.

21  *Reader's Digest*, October 1991, p 61.

22  From 'Words of Love By Mother Teresa' in *Education for Democracy*, Benjamin R. Barber and Richard M. Battistoni, Editors (Dubuque: Kendall / Hunt Publishing Company, 1993).

23  Ibid.

24  *White Fang*, Jack London (New York: Tom Doherty Associates, Inc., 1988).

25  Ibid.

26  Swindoll, *Hand Me Another Brick* (Thomas Nelson, 1978) pp 82, 88.

27  Ibid.

28  'Christmas at Home', P. W. Alexander, in *Writing for Change: A Community Reader* (San Francisco, CA: McGraw-Hill, Inc., 1995) pp 100, 101.

29  Ibid. p 102.

30  Author Unknown.

31  'The Endless Streetcar Ride into the Night, and the Tinfoil Noose', Jean Shepherd, in *The Riverside Reader*, Vol. 1 (Boston, MA: Houghton Mifflin Company, 1985) p 32.

32  Ibid., p 37.

33  Ibid.

34  Ibid., p 17.

35  Meryle Secrest, *Leonard Bernstein: A Life* (Knopf, 1995).

36  *Common Ground*, January 1990.

37  'Mending Walls', Robert Frost, in *Writing for Change: A Community Reader* (San Francisco, CA: McGraw-Hill, Inc, 1995) pp 123–124.

38  *Who Said That?* George Sweeting (Chicago, IL: Moody Press, 1995).

39  *Teaching and Learning in Communities of Faith*, Linda J. Vogel (San Francisco, CA: Jossey-Bass Publishers, 1991) p 124.

40  Doug Lipman, The Hasidic Stories Home Page (http://hasidic.storypower.com), 1996.

41  Ansel Adams, *Morning Edition* November 24 1997 (National Public Radio).

42  Ibid.

43  Author Unknown.

44  'Churchill, Sir Winston Leonard Spencer', *Microsoft® Encarta® 98 Encyclopedia*. © 1993–1997 Microsoft Corporation. All rights reserved.

45  Ibid.

46  *Who Said That?* George Sweeting (Chicago, IL: Moody Press, 1995).

47  *Reader's Digest*, January 1999, pp 58–61.

Other devotional books offered by Eagle
Publishing are:

*God's Little Devotional Book*
*God's Little Devotional Book for Couples*
*God's Little Devotional Book for Fathers*
*God's Little Devotional Book for Graduates*
*God's Little Devotional Book for Men*
*God's Little Devotional Book for Mothers*
*God's Little Devotional Book for Students*
*God's Little Devotional Book for Teens*
*God's Little Devotional Book for Women*

Also

*God's little Lessons on Life*
*God's little Lessons for Fathers*
*God's little Lessons for Mothers*

*Through the Night with God*